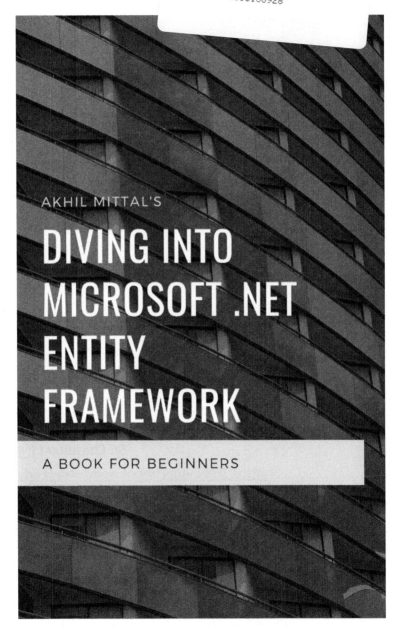

AKHIL MITTAL'S

DIVING INTO MICROSOFT .NET ENTITY FRAMEWORK

A BOOK FOR BEGINNERS

©2018 Akhil Mittal (www.codeteddy.com)

DIVING into MICROSOFT .NET ENTITY FRAMEWORK
(A Practical Approach of Learning Entity Framework)

Akhil Mittal
Sr. Consultant (Magic EdTech)
https://www.facebook.com/codeteddydotcom/
https://in.linkedin.com/in/akhilmittal
https://twitter.com/AkhilMittal20
google.com/+AkhilMittal
https://www.codeteddy.com
https://github.com/akhilmittal

About Author

Akhil Mittal is two times Microsoft MVP (Most Valuable Professional), C# Corner MVP, Codeproject MVP, a blogger, author and likes to write/read technical articles. Akhil has an experience of around 12 years in developing, designing, architecting enterprise level applications primarily in Microsoft Technologies. Akhil enjoys working on technologies like MVC, Web API, Entity Framework, Angular, C#, and Blockchain. Akhil is an MCP (Microsoft Certified Professional) in Web Applications and Dot Net Framework. Visit Akhil Mittal's personal blog CodeTeddy (https://codeteddy.com) for some good and informative articles.

(AKHIL MITTAL)

Preface

The intent of this book is to explain the basics of Entity Framework and the three data access approaches that Microsoft's Entity Framework provides. This book covers the introduction to Entity Framework, how Entity Framework's capabilities could be leveraged in .Net development irrespective of the type of application used, the key features of Entity Framework, what are the areas where Entity Framework could be used as an ORM and the history of Entity Framework. The book talks about various data access techniques that could be achieved using Entity Framework and use of code first migrations in Entity Framework. The querying options and various loading options of Entity Framework are explained with examples. The book also talks about the introduction to Entity Framework Core and its implementation details. The book would be more practical in nature thereby covering a less of theory and explaining the data access approaches in Entity Framework 6 and Entity Framework Core in any .Net application. The book chapters are in a tutorial format and showcase small data access applications using Entity Framework for the sake of understanding the concept. Once the concept and key capabilities of Entity Framework and Entity Framework Core are understood, those could be applied in any application based on need and requirement.

Table of Contents

What is Entity Framework

Microsoft Entity Framework is an ORM (Object-relational mapping). The definition from Wikipedia is very straightforward for ORM and pretty much self-explanatory,

"Object-relational mapping (ORM, O/RM, and O/R mapping tool) in computer science is a programming technique for converting data between incompatible type systems using object-oriented programming languages. This creates, in effect, a "virtual object database" that can be used from within the programming language. "

Entity Framework is an Object Relational Mapper, which we regularly allude to as an ORM, and what an ORM does is it disentangles the exertion that we need to make when we're trying to persist the objects in our application in the database. The responsibilities that the ORM will deal with for us are making associations, and connections, executing commands on the database. Entity Framework also takes care of the results of the queries performed on the database, it reads the data and takes care of instances of entity/model classes and push/ pulls the data from the database. So, in a nutshell, all the repetitive tasks that a developer or an application would perform while working with legacy data access approaches would be handled by Entity Framework as an ORM. Entity Framework as we call it an ORM is a Microsoft's product that is now an integral part of .Net development stack. ORM's major capability is to directly map the domain classes or model classes to the database schema and a domain class typically act as a reflection of a related table in the database. Entity Framework acts much smarter than the typical ORM's, it allows a lot more flexibility between the database schema and the domain classes. It gives the flexibility to even design the domain classes in a manner that makes more sense to the business domain or a database schema could be designed in a way that makes it more effective as a database for the domain for which it is designed. It takes care of all the mapping part and does not force the developer or underlying application to manually define mappings. Entity Framework by default comes along with some smart assumptions and settings but those settings are flexible enough to be overwritten as per application needs. It simplifies developers and applications job to explicitly take care or repetitive data operations and eliminates the complexities and learning curve to understand the abstraction of how database operations are done.

Why Entity Framework

Being an ORM, Entity Framework is a data access framework provided by Microsoft that helps to establish a relation between objects and data structure in the application. It is built over traditional ADO.NET and acts as a wrapper over ADO.NET and is an enhancement over ADO.NET that provided data access in more automated way thereby reducing a developer's effort to struggle with connections, data readers or data sets. It is an abstraction over all those and is more powerful w.r.t. the offerings it makes. A developer can have more control over what data he needs, in which form and how much. Entity Framework provides a dependable API, so software developers can focus on solving their business problems, not worry about solving the problems of data persistence. A developer having no database development background or not very intimate knowledge of databases can leverage Entity framework's along with LINQ capabilities to write an optimized query to perform DB operations.

Since it dispenses with a vast number of repetitive information association assignments, Entity Framework can upgrade a developer's efficiency. It likewise gives consistency in the undertakings it does, instead of having different colleagues of any team having their own methods for data access. Entity Framework, of course, has its own learning curve especially if you need to understand it in deeper to leverage its advanced features but that learning curve is quick since the technology is very interesting.

The SQL or DB query execution would be handled by Entity Framework in the background and it will take care of all the transactions and concurrency issues that may occur.

Relational Model and Object Model

Object-Relational Mapping is a strategy that gives you a chance to query and control/manipulate data from a database utilizing an object-oriented paradigm. Therefore, in our code, we can chip away at objects as opposed to straightforwardly composing SQL proclamations. Relational models and object models don't work extremely well together. A relational database chooses the tabular format to represent the data and OO languages represent it as an interconnected graph of objects. It's the ORM library that implements the object-relational mapping technique, like Entity Framework, that takes care of this. In most of the basic scenarios, those objects directly map to the database tables. But I larger applications and complex scenarios, this OO technique allows implementing OO functionality like inheritance. A base Person class and an Employee class that inherits person can map to data stored in the same table in the database. Or better granularity without inheritance, a table in a database might translate to a separate set of classes in an OO model. The entities the ORM works with are different than a 1 on 1 mapping to tables.

Entity Framework History

Most programming that we make utilizes information and we need to store in the database, and at some points recover the same information to show it to end users, allow end users to access, modify or add new data or information. These undertakings are generally secondary to the issues we're attempting to settle when building programming, yet for quite a long time we invested strange measures of effort composing code just to get information all through our information store or best to be called a database. Over those years, Microsoft, too, has experienced various emphases of getting information via APIs. ActiveX Data Objects, or ADO, was around for quite a while and it, in the long run, progressed toward becoming ADO.NET, yet ADO ADO.NET still expected us to be exceptionally associated with creating connections and commands in converting database query results into understandable entities, being mindful of the creation of our databases, and that's only the tip of the iceberg. In 2008 Microsoft moved its data access strategy to object-relational mapper having an automated involvement with relational databases and making it possible to translate the objects to and from the raw data. This does not require a developer to have an intense knowledge of database or its schema. This innovation was named as Entity Framework and it became the Microsoft's primary data access API. This API evolved over years and then the most stable version i.e. EF 6 came out which has more than 48,062,308 downloads and more so far. The current version is 6.2.0 which has 3,785,701 and more downloads so far. Let's have a glance over the history of Entity Framework.

1. Entity Framework's first version came out with .Net Framework 3.5 SP1 with VS 2008 SP1 on 11th August 2008. This version was not at all accepted by the developers.

2. The second version i.e. EF4 (Entity Framework 4.0) was part of .Net Framework 4.0 that was released on 12th April 2010 that evolved drastically from its first version.

3. Soon, the third version named EF 4.1 was released on 12th April 2011 having Code First Approach and following that a new update to the same version was released on 25th July 2011 that supported new types and fixed prior bugs. This version was widely accepted.

4. An updated version EF 4.3.1 came out on February 29th, 2012 that had support for migrations as well.

5. On August 11th, 2010 version 5.0.0 was released targeting .Net Framework 4.5 which was made available for .net Framework 4.0 as well.

6. On 17th October 2013, Microsoft released Entity Framework's version 6.0 which was made an open source and its source code was made available at Git. It has a drastic improvement over code first approach of data access.

7. Aligning to the Microsoft's vision of modernizing the components and make them more cross-platform to run on Linux or any other platform like OSX, they release Entity Framework Core 1.0 on 27th June 2016 along with Asp.Net Core 1.0. Microsoft didn't upgrade the earlier version of EF, rather launched a new one as earlier might be a complete rewrite to support Core components.

8. On 14th August 2017 with VS 2017 EF Core 2.0 was released with ASP.NET Core 2.0

How Entity Framework Can Benefit an Application

Though Entity Framework has a lot of offerings but in real life scenarios, how well can it be fitted in applications? Let's take a real-time scenario. Assume a web application initially been written using traditional Asp.Net having ADO.NET approach of data access. Imagine the kind of issues it may face. It has a development time maintaining SQL connections and commands, it cannot expand to any new database apart from SQL, there would be an additional development effort to transform the raw data to the desired model or entities, a developer needs to have a sound database knowledge along with knowing the schema of the database, the database objects are directly exposed within the code, the data access operations would be very tightly coupled and specific to the database used i.e. SQL. Now using Entity Framework all these could be easily achieved in an application, no matter it is an enterprise level or a basic application. For e.g. a company had an enterprise level product to convert pdf into books supporting all the document formats and providing editing features as well. The product was written in Asp.Net with ADO.Net. Their requirement was to scale up, so they chose Entity Framework as it also provided the software the flexibility to write microservices with independent databases for the services having their own contexts. The database was varied from SQL, to My SQL to Oracle or all the three databases could be used at the same time with Entity Framework thereby having separate contexts and no code change at all. These offerings make EF stronger.

Entity Framework could be therefore also used in the scenarios where in a typical application the UI and data access code are tightly bound. This is one perspective and not the only place where one can use Entity Framework. It addresses all the problems that restricted the typical ASP.Net application with ADO.NET application to scale up. EF facilitates the way to know which domain object will work in a model. This could be defined by a separate context. In Entity Framework that is called DbContext. An application can have more than on DbContexts to be used independently in the big software as per need. It handles the objects, state, and the relation of the entities along with the persistence of the data. DbContext takes responsibilities of executing LINQ and tracking the in-memory changes as well. This also proves to be an abstraction of Entity Framework to be directly known by an application which is of course not at all needed.

Entity Framework Architecture

The following image shows the architecture of the Entity Framework over ADO.NET.

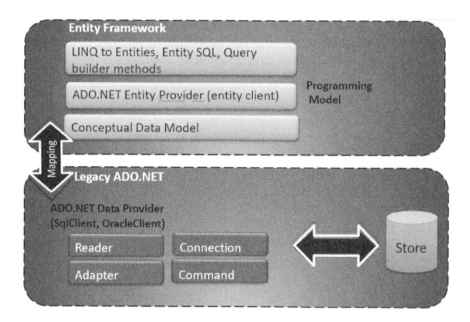

The picture clearly defines that Entity Framework is a wrapper over legacy ADO.NET with more powerful features. Legacy ADO.NET had the overhead of maintaining connections, commands, readers and adapters to interact with the database or data store whereas Entity Framework has an internal mapping with these technicalities thus refraining developer to have direct access over those and focus on domain and entities. The EF structure has a Conceptual Data Model that could be used by end application like services, APIs or any other client. This facilitates application to have access to domain classes and mappings whereas storage model is abstracted and kept part of EF implementation only. LINQ to SQL or Entity SQL could be used for querying the data. Entity SQL is a bit tricky and has its own learning curve.

Following image shows the Entity Framework Architecture.

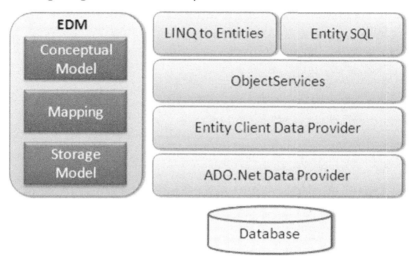

Image credit: http://www.entityframeworktutorial.net/EntityFramework-Architecture.aspx

Let's look at the components of the architecture individually.

EDM (Entity Data Model): Entity Data Model consists of mainly three parts i.e. Conceptual Storage Definition language(CSDL), Storage Schema Definition Language(SSDL) and Mapping Schema Definition Language (MSDL).

CSDL: CSDL defines the domain classes and relationships between those, these are pure C# code and are exposed to end client and are independent of the database schema. These could be used by any application, API or service to access the underlying domain and their relationships.

SSDL: SSDL is mainly focussed on defining the database schema i.e. it contains the details of tables, functions, stored procedures, relationships, keys, and constraints. It is stored in the form of an XML having all these information from the database.

MSDL: The role of MSDL is to define the mapping between CSDL and SSDL. It ensures that the conceptual model is mapped with the storage model so that any transaction with the conceptual model directly result in the impacting database due to this mapping.

LINQ to Entities (L2E): This is a well-known and well-used query language technique used by developers to write queries against domain model or CSDL classes. It is purely LINQ and entities from CSDL are returned as the result while using it.

Entity SQL: Entity SQL can only be used with EF 6. This is also a query language like L2E but has a learning curve to understand and implement. L2E is comparatively more convenient to use.

Object Service: Object Service defines the actual entry point for all the database transactions and operations. It is responsible for converting the raw data into domain object structure i.e. materialization.

Entity Client Data Provider: The entity client data provider's main responsibilities are to convert L2E or Entity SQL data access queries to queries that could be understood by the database for e.g. if SQL Server is used then to SQL queries. It is the one which communicates with the ADO.Net data provider internally and that in turn communicates with the database in the traditional approach to fetch or save the data.

ADO.Net Data Provider: This layer communicates with the actual database for all the operations in the traditional way.

Entity Framework Approaches

It is very common to know the three approaches that Microsoft Entity Framework provides. The three approaches are as follows,

1. Model First
2. Database First and
3. Code First
   (i) Generate database from data model classes.
   (ii) Generate data model classes from existing database.

The model first approach says that we have a model with all kind of entities and relations/associations using which we can generate a database that will eventually have entities and properties converted into database tables and columns and associations and relations would be converted into foreign keys respectively.

Database First approach says that we already have an existing database and we need to access that database in our application. We can create an entity data model along with its relations ship directly from the database with just a few clicks and start accessing the database from our code. All the entities i.e. classes would be generated by Entity Framework that could be used in applications data access layer to participate in DB operation queries.

The code first approach is the recommended approach with EF especially when you are starting the development of an application from scratch. You can define the POCO classes in advance and their relationships and envision how your database structure and data model may look like by just defining the structure in the code. Entity framework, at last, will take all the responsibility to generate a database for you for your POCO classes and data model and will take care of transactions, history, and migrations.

With all the three approaches you have full control over updating the database and code as per need at any point in time.

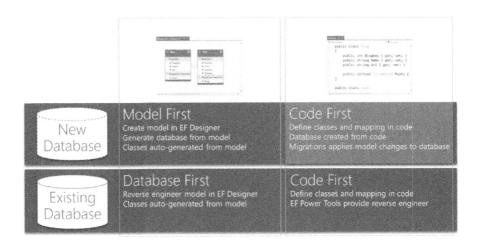

Model First

Using model first approach a developer may not need to write any code for generating a database. Entity Framework provides the designer tools that could help you make a model and then generate a database out of it. The tools are more of a drag and drop controls that just need inputs like what your entity name is, what properties it should have, how it is related to other entities and so. The user interface is very easy to use and interesting. Model designer when good to go will help you to generate DDL commands that could be directly executed from Visual Studio or on your database server to create a database out of your created model. This creates an EDMX file that stores the information of your conceptual model, storage model and mapping between both. To learn about the conceptual model and storage model, you can refer to the link I provided in the introduction of this article. The only drawback that I can see is that dropping the database completely and recreating it would be a challenge with this approach.

Database First

We use database first approach when we already have an existing database and need to access that in our application. Establishing the data access methodology for existing database with Entity Framework will help us to generate the context and classes in our solution through which we can access the database. It is opposite of model first approach, here model is created via database and we have full control to choose what tables to include in the model, what, stored procedures, functions or views to include. Your application may be a sub-application that does not need all the tables or objects of your big database, so you can have liberty here to control what you want in your application and what not. Whenever the database schema changes, you can easily update the entity data model by just one click in the designer or entity data model and that will take care of mapping and create necessary classes in your application.

Code First

Using code first approach, a developer's focus is only on code and not on database or data model. The developer can define classes and their mapping in the code itself and since now Entity Framework supports inheritance, it is easier to define relationships. Entity framework takes care of creating or re-creating database for you and not only this while creating a database, you can provide seed data i.e. master data that you want your tables should have when the database is created. Using code first, you may not have a .edmx file with relationships and schema as it does not depend upon Entity Framework designer and its tools and would have more control over the database since you are the one who created classes and relationships and managing it. There is a new concept of code first migrations that came up which makes code first approach easier to use and follow, but in this article, I'll not use migrations but old method of creating DB context and DB set classes so that you understand what is under the hood. Code first approach could also be used to generate code from an existing database, so basically it offers two methods in which it could be used.

Entity Framework Approaches in Action

Enough of theory, let's start with the implementation part one by one and step by step to explore and learn each approach. I'll use sample project and that too a console application to connect with the database using Entity Framework for all the three approaches. I'll use basic sample tables to explain the concept. The intent here is to learn the concept and implement it and not to create a large application. When you learn it, you can use the concepts with any large enterprise level application or any big database server which can have thousands of tables. So, we'll follow the KISS strategy and keep it simple here.

Model First

1. Create a simple .Net Framework console application by opening your visual studio and choosing the console application template. We can choose any application type like a web application that could be ASP.NET web forms, MVC or Web API or windows application/WPF application. You can give a name to the project and solution of your choice.

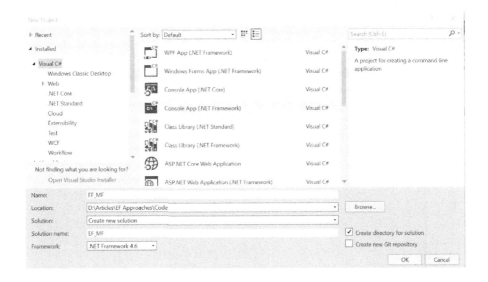

2. We'll have Program.cs, the only class and App.config in our project.

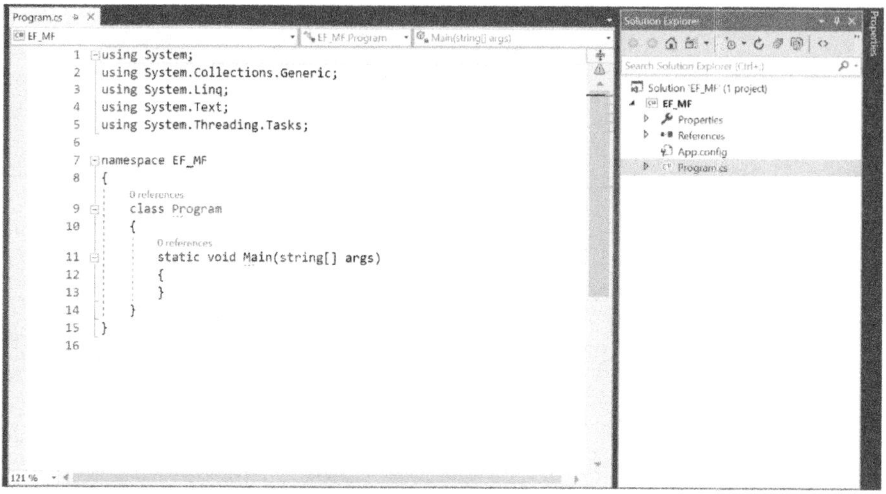

3. Right-click the project and click on add a new item, this will open the window to add a new item, just go to Data as shown in below image and choose ADO.NET Entity Data Model as shown in the following image. Give it a name for e.g. EFModel and click on Add.

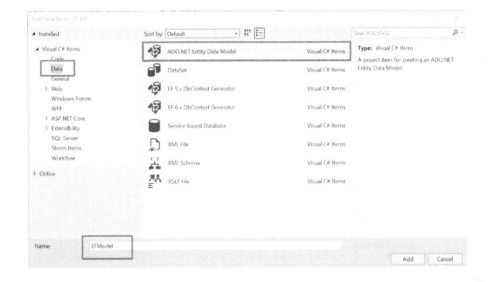

4. Once you click add, you'll be shown to choose Model Contents, and this is the place where you choose what approach you want to use for data access out of the three EF approaches. So, choose Empty EF Designer because we would be using model first approach and create a model from scratch.

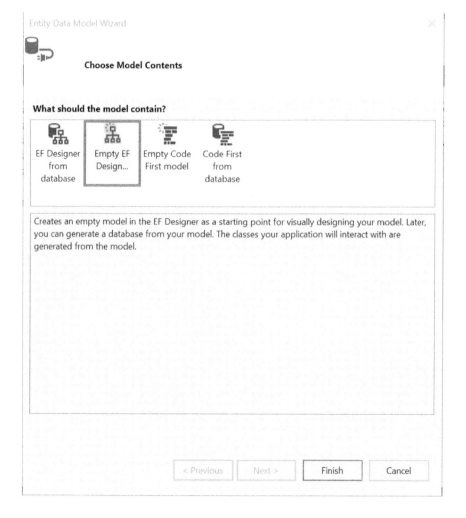

5. Once you click "Finish", you see the empty designer window that is the .edmx file. The name of the .edmx file in solution is the name that we provided while adding the EF designer model. In the toolbox, you see the tools available that you could use to create entities and associations between them.

6. Drag and drop the Entity tool from the toolbox into the designer. It will create an empty entity as shown below with one property named Id, saying it is a primary key. Here you can rename the entity and add more scalar properties.

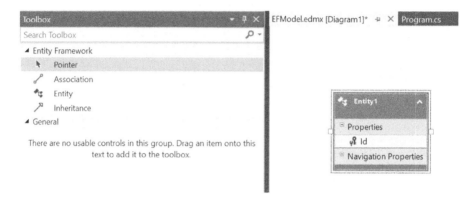

7. Right click on entity created and add a new scalar property as shown in the following image. Rename the name of the entity from Entity1 to Student. You can rename the entity by double-clicking on the entity name and right click and rename the entity.

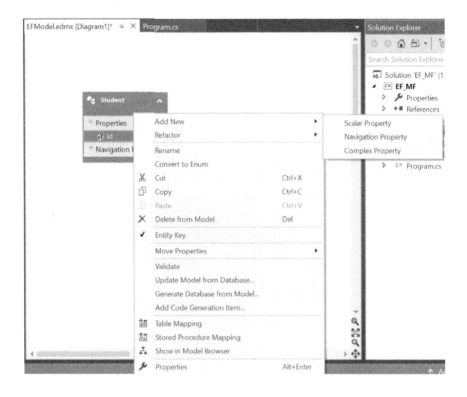

8. Name the scalar property as "Name".

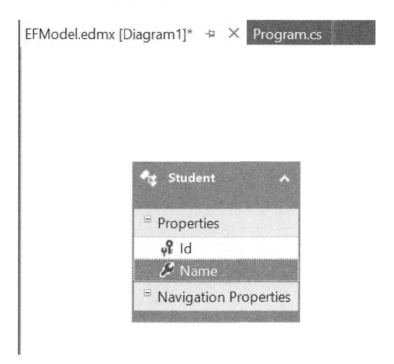

9. In an analogous way add a new entity named Class and add a new property named ClassName. We here are trying to create a student and a class relationship where a class can have multiple students. So, we have an option to choose Association from toolbox as shown below and drag the Association tool from Class to Student and it showed 1 to many relationship.

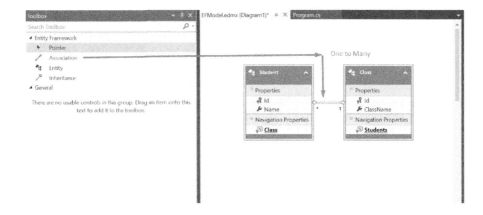

10. We are not adding more entities and try to understand the basic functionality of these two entities. Right click on the designer and click on "Generate Database from Model..." option to generate the scripts.

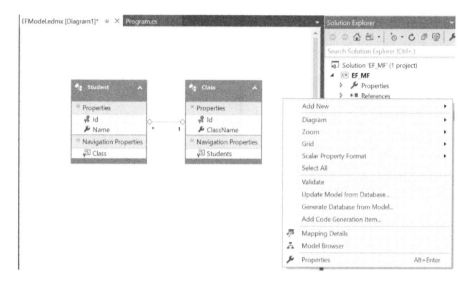

11. Once you click on "Generate Database from Model..." option, you'll be asked to choose data connection as shown in the following window. You can choose a new connection or an existing one. I'll choose a new connection but before that, I'll create an empty database on my SQL server so that I do not have to modify my scripts to provide a database name. By default, the generated scrips create tables in the master database if DB name is not specified.

12. Open your SQL Server and create a new database and name it as per your choice. I am naming it StudentDB as shown in the following images.

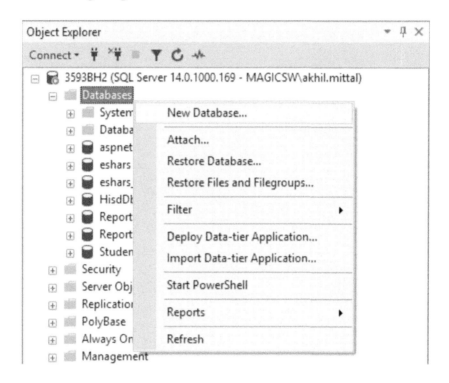

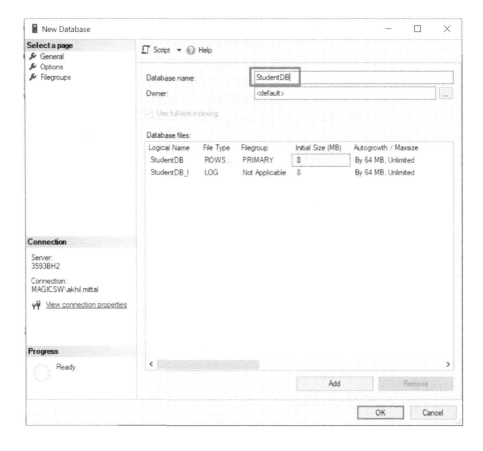

13. Coming back to the window where we needed to provide the connection details. Choose your data source and server name as shown in the following image. The server name should be the server where you created the empty database. Now in the selecting database option, expand the dropdown and you should see your database name. Select the database name.

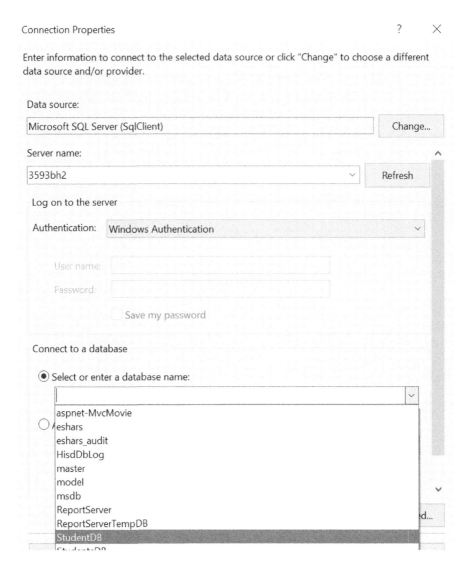

14. Once you select the database name, a connection string would be generated as shown below and it will say that the connection string would be saved I the App.Config file with the name EFModelContainer. EFModelContainer is the name of the connection string. Since it is an EF generated connection string, you see it has the information about EF CSDL, MSL and SSDL files as well that would be present in our application. Click Next to proceed.

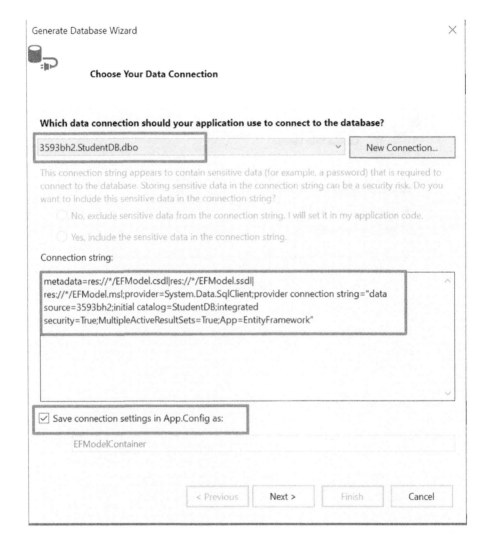

15. Next step is to choose your Entity Framework version. We'll use 6.x i.e. it will automatically pick the latest stable version with EF6. Click Next.

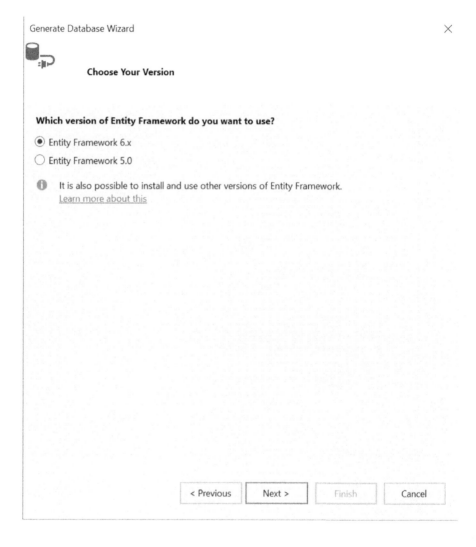

As a last step of the wizard, you'll see the needed SQL scripts created for us. You can choose to rename the scripts but by default, it takes the name as <model name>.edmx.sql. I'll leave it as it is and click Finish to proceed.

You'll see the script located in solution explorer now. Double click to open it and it opens in a window where you have an option to directly execute it.

16. Before executing the scripts let's first install Entity Framework latest stable version from the Nuget package manager. It is very simple to do. Go to Tools in Visual Studio, then choose NuGet Package Manager->Package Manager Console as shown in the following image.

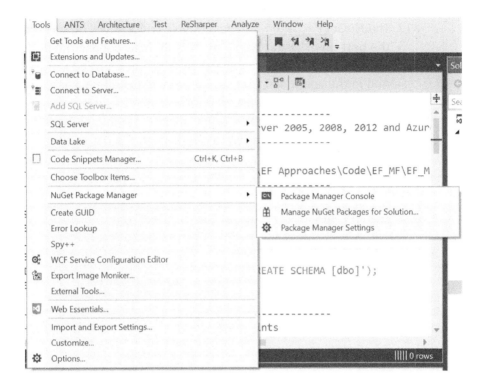

17. The NuGet Package Manager console window will be opened at the bottom of Visual Studio by default. Now choose the project for which the Entity Framework package needs to be installed. And in the command that says PM> type **Install-Package EntityFramework** and press enter. We do not specify the version of Entity Framework as we want the latest stable package should be downloaded and added to our project as a DLL reference.

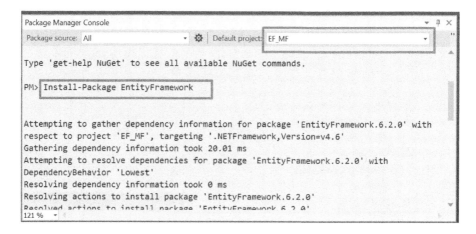

18. Once done with installing Entity Framework, go back to the script window and on the top left, you see the button to execute the scripts as shown below. Press the button to execute the scripts.

```
EFModel.edmx.sql    ⚏ ✕  EFModel.edmx [Diagram1]          Program.cs

▷ ▾  ⊟  ✓  ▤    ▥▤  ▥  ▥                          ▾  ⚏  ▤  ▾  ⚏  ▥

 ▷   Execute                     Ctrl+Shift+E
 ▷   Execute With Debugger                      --------------------------------
    3    -- Entity Designer DDL Script for SQL Server 2005, 2008, 2012 and Azur
    4    -- --------------------------------------------------
    5    -- Date Created: 07/26/2018 15:58:32
    6    -- Generated from EDMX file: D:\Articles\EF Approaches\Code\EF_MF\EF_M
    7    -- --------------------------------------------------
    8
    9    SET QUOTED_IDENTIFIER OFF;
   10    GO
   11    USE [StudentDB];
   12    GO
   13    IF SCHEMA_ID(N'dbo') IS NULL EXECUTE(N'CREATE SCHEMA [dbo]');
   14    GO
   15
   16  ⊟ -- --------------------------------------------------
   17    -- Dropping existing FOREIGN KEY constraints
   18    -- --------------------------------------------------
   19
   20
   21    -- --------------------------------------------------
   22    -- Dropping existing tables
   23    -- --------------------------------------------------
121 %   ▾  ◀                                                           ▶
```

19. Once you click on Execute, a new window will show up asking server and database details. Fill in the details specific to your server and database as shown below and click Connect.

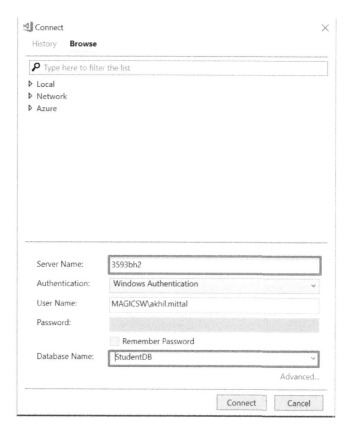

20. Once done, go to your database server and you'll see the tables are created for our database StudentDB. The names of the tables are pluralized, and Student table has a foreign key reference to Classes table and the foreign key is automatically created named Class_Id referencing Classes table. It is magical, isn't it?

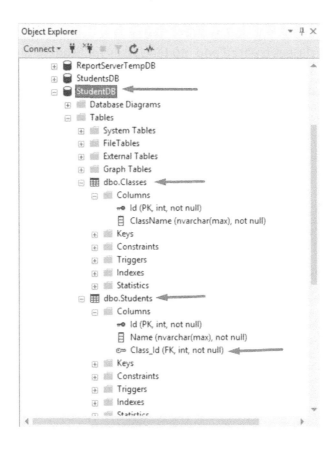

21. In our solution explorer, we see the .edmx file and the context classes created and model classes for Student and Class entities. This is all done in the background by EF designer. So, till now we did not write a single code and got all the code generated by EF.

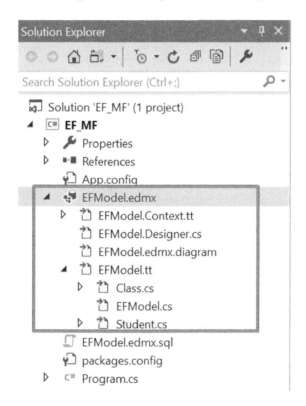

22. Open the EFModel.Context.cs class file and we see the name of the DbContext class that got generated is EFModelContainer. Remember that is the name of our connection string stored in App.Config. The name of the context class has to be the same as connection string name for EF to know the relation. So, you can have multiple DB context classes in the same solution with different names and pointing to different connection strings. You

can explore more on DbContext class and what other ways you can make its relation to the connection string in the config file. One another way is to call its base constructor by passing name of the connection string as a parameter to its parameterized constructor. But for the sake of understanding, we'll stick to this implementation.

23. Now it's time to test our implementation and check if the Entity Framework is actually working and helping us in database operations or not. So, in the Program.cs class's Main method we'll try to write some code that saves a new class for us in the database. Create a new object of EFModelContainer and in the container, we get the entity classes collection coming from DbContext. Add a new Class. The class is the name of the entity class generated for us via designer. And name the class as "Nursery". We do not have to specify the id attribute for the class, as EF will automatically handle this and provide an Id to a newly added record. The code to add a new class named "Nursery" is shown in the following image. The container.SaveChanges statement is the statement when executed will add a new record in the database for us.

```
App.config        EFModel.edmx.sql        EFModel.edmx [Diagram1]        Program.cs  ₽ ×
C# EF_MF                                                                    ▾  EF_MF.Program
    4    using System.Text;
    5    using System.Threading.Tasks;
    6
    7  □namespace EF_MF
    8    {
             0 references
    9  □      class Program
   10         {
                 0 references
   11  □          static void Main(string[] args)
   12             {
   13                 EFModelContainer container = new EFModelContainer();
   14                 container.Classes.Add(new Class() {ClassName = "Nursery"});
   15                 container.SaveChanges();
   16             }
   17         }
   18    }
```

24. Just run the application and let the main method code execute. Once done, go to your database and check the Classes table, you'll see a new record is added in the Classes table with the class name "Nursery" which is what we provided while wanted to add a

record. So, it works ▢. Notice the Id that is auto generated by Entity Framework.

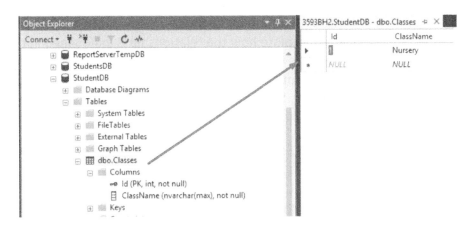

25. Now, let's try something new and try to add a new class but this time with students. We have a relationship of class with students that is a class can have many students and a student will belong to one class. Check the created model classes for Student and Class if you want to explore how the relationship is maintained in the classes. So, this time, we'll add a new class and add some students to that class. Entity Framework should automatically add these students to the Students table and make the relationship with the Class table. Following is the simple self-explanatory code for doing this.

```
static void Main(string[] args)
{
    EFModelContainer container = new
EFModelContainer();
    ICollection<Student> students = new
List<Student>
    {
        new Student() { Name = "Mark" },
        new Student() { Name = "Joe" },
        new Student() { Name = "Allen" }
    };

    container.Classes.Add(new Class()
{ClassName = "KG", Students = students });
    container.SaveChanges();
}
```

In the above code, we create an EFModelContainer object and a list of Students by adding three students into it. Now add a new class to the container object, just like we did in the last example and assign students to the Students property of the Class object. Last but not the least, container.SaveChanges().

```
namespace EF_MF
{
    0 references
    class Program
    {
        0 references
        static void Main(string[] args)
        {
            EFModelContainer container = new EFModelContainer();
            ICollection<Student> students = new List<Student>
            {
                new Student() { Name = "Mark" },
                new Student() { Name = "Joe" },
                new Student() { Name = "Allen" }
            };

            container.Classes.Add(new Class() {ClassName = "KG", Students = students });
            container.SaveChanges();
        }
    }
}
```

26. Run the code and go to the database. Check the Classes table and see a newly created class row with name "KG" that we supplied from the code.

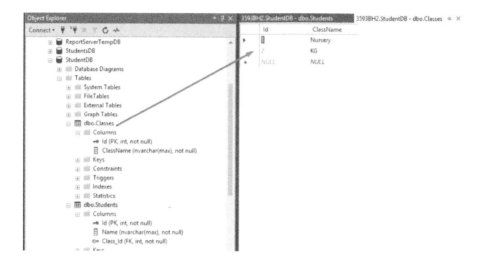

Now, go to the Students table and we got three students created there those we supplied from code and check the Class_Id column that has the foreign key reference to the newly created class with Id 2. Amazing [?]

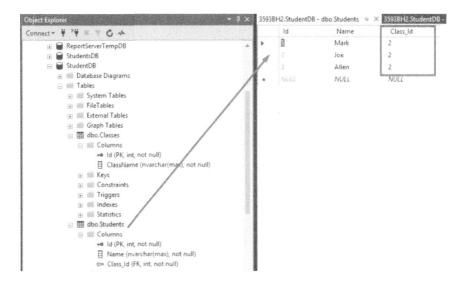

Like this, you can perform complex queries and other CRUD operations on your database by writing simple code. Try to perform more operations like editing, deleting fetching the records to understand more. Let's move to our next topic that is database first approach with Entity Framework.

Database First

1. Like we did in model first approach, create a new console application and name it EF_DBF.

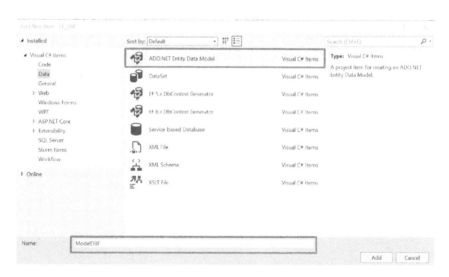

2. The second step is to add a new ADO.NET Entity Data Model to this project. Name it of your choice. I named it ModelDBF.

3. Now, from the choose model window, we'll choose the option of EFDesigner from the database, this will help us to create an Entity Framework designer from the existing database.

4. Next, choose the connection for the database, i.e provide the details on the wizard for your existing database. I'll take the database we created with our model first approach i.e. StudentDB. Once we choose the database, we see the Entity Framework connection string and the name of the connection string to be saved in App.Config i.e. StudentDBEntities. You can also change it if you want. Click Next.

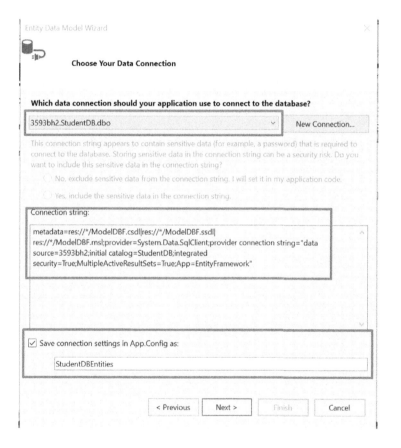

5. Choose the EF version. I already explained the meaning of 6.x. We'll choose the same and click Next.

©2018 Akhil Mittal (www.codeteddy.com)

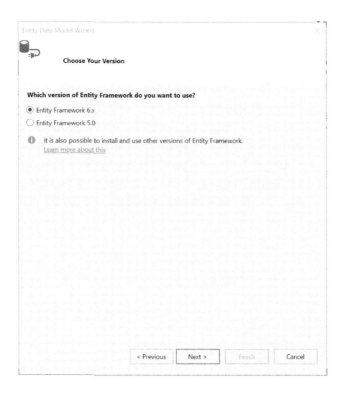

6. Now in this step, you would be shown all the database objects related to the database you selected initially, and it is your choice to include or exclude the objects you need. The objects could be tables, views or stored procedures. Since we do not have views and stored procedures, we'll only choose our two tables as shown in the following image. Since we already have the table's name in pluralized forms, I do not want to complicate this by again pluralizing it and appending one more 's' to my entity classes, so I unchecked that option of pluralizing the entity names. Provide model namespace or leave it as it is with the default name provided and click Finish.

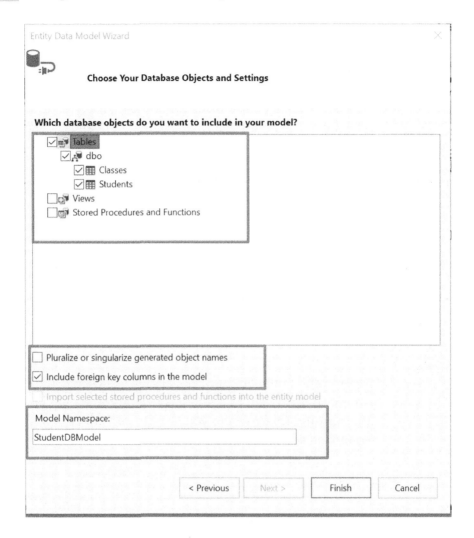

7. Once you click Finish, you see the entities created in the EF designer for the database objects we selected from the database. We notice that it is like what we had when we manually created the entities and generated a database out of it. This EF designer also takes care of foreign key relationship and shows the one to many association between class and student entities.

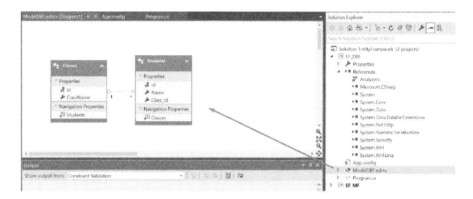

8. Time to add Entity Framework package like we did in the first approach discussed. Make sure you choose the right project i.e. the current project where you need to add EF. Type the command in package manager Console and press enter.

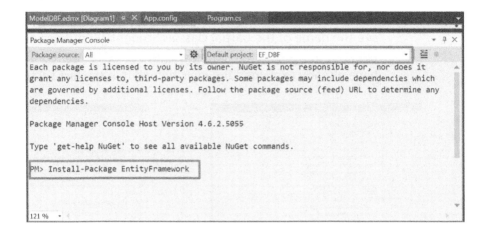

9. Now, when we open the generated ModelDBF.Context.cs, we
    see the name of the partial class as StudentDBEntities i.e. the
    name of the connection string we got stored in App.Config. I
    have already explained the logic behind it in the last section.

10. Time to see some action now. Add the code below to the Program.cs Main() method.

```
static void Main(string[] args)
        {
            StudentDBEntities container = new
StudentDBEntities();
            ICollection<Students> students = new
List<Students>
                {
                    new Students() { Name = "Harry" },
                    new Students() { Name = "Jane" },
                    new Students() { Name = "Nick" }
                };

            container.Classes.Add(new Classes() {
ClassName = "Class 1", Students = students });
            container.SaveChanges();

            container.Students.Add(new Students()
{Class_Id = 1, Name = "Ben"});
            container.SaveChanges();

        }
```

In the above code, we are trying to create an object of StudentDBEntities class i.e. our context class and a collection of students to be added to our database. To check the relationship is working fine or not, we'll add a new class named "Class 1" and assign the Students property to our students collection and SaveChanges() again to check if individual student insertion is working or not, we'll add a new student named "Ben" to the Students model and assign the class id to 1 i.e. the existing class we have in database and SaveChanges(). Put a breakpoint in Main method and press F5.

```csharp
namespace EF_DBF
{
    class Program
    {
        static void Main(string[] args)
        {
            StudentDBEntities container = new StudentDBEntities();
            ICollection<Students> students = new List<Students>
            {
                new Students() { Name = "Harry" },
                new Students() { Name = "Jane" },
                new Students() { Name = "Nick" }
            };

            container.Classes.Add(new Classes() { ClassName = "Class 1", Students = students });
            container.SaveChanges();

            container.Students.Add(new Students() {Class_Id = 1, Name = "Ben"});
            container.SaveChanges();
        }
    }
}
```

11. When the application runs it will hit the breakpoint. Navigate through the statements by pressing F10 and stop at line 24 i.e. before we add a new student. Since we already executed the code for saving changes for newly added class. Let's go to the database and check.

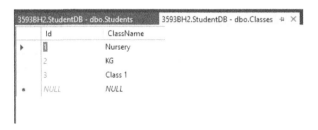

12. In the database, we see the newly added class has a new row in Classes table with ID 3.

Id	ClassName
1	Nursery
2	KG
3	Class 1
NULL	NULL

And in the Students table, we see that three students that we added from code got inserted in the table with the class id as 3 i.e. the newly created class.

3593BH2.StudentDB - dbo.Students			3593BH2.StudentDB - dbo.Classe
Id	Name	Class_Id	
1	Mark	2	
2	Joe	2	
3	Allen	2	
4	Harry	3	
5	Jane	3	
6	Nick	3	
NULL	NULL	NULL	

13. Now get back to Visual Studio and execute the line for adding a new student.

```
container.Students.Add(new Students() {Class_Id = 1, Name = "Ben"});
container.SaveChanges();   DbContext.SaveChanges() = 1
```

Once done, check the database and we see a new student having the name "Ben" added to our Students table having Class_Id 1 that we assigned in code.

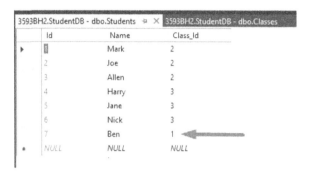

We see our database first approach also working fine. Again, you can try other DB operations in the code at your will and play with the code to explore more. Let's move on to code first approach.

Code First

1. Create a new console application named EF_CF. This will give you Program.cs and a Main() method inside that.

```csharp
using System;
using System.Collections.Generic;
using System.Linq;
using System.Text;
using System.Threading.Tasks;

namespace EF_CF
{
    class Program
    {
        static void Main(string[] args)
        {
        }
    }
}
```

2. We'll create our model classes now i.e. POCO (Plain Old CLR Object) classes. Let's say we have to create an application where there would be database operations for an employee and an employee would be allocated to some department. So, A department can have multiple employees and an employee will have only one department. So, we'll create the first two entities, Employee, and Department. Add a new class to the project named Employee and add two simple properties to it i.e. EmployeeId and EmployeeName.

```
Employee.cs*  ×  Program.cs      Program.cs      App.config      Program.cs
EF_CF                              ▼  EF_CF Employee      ▼  EmployeeName
    3    using System.Linq;
    4    using System.Text;
    5    using System.Threading.Tasks;
    6
    7   □namespace EF_CF
    8    {
             0 references
    9        public class Employee
   10        {
                 0 references
   11            public int EmployeeId { get; set; }
                 0 references
   12            public string EmployeeName { get; set; }
   13        }
   14    }
```

Solution Explorer

Search Solution Explorer (Ctrl+;)

Solution 'EntityFramework' (3 pr
  ▲ EF_CF
    ▷ 🔧 Properties
    ▷ ■ References
        App.config
    ▷ Employee.cs
    ▷ Program.cs
  ▷ EF_DBF
  ▷ EF_MF

3. Similarly, add a new class named Department and add properties DepartmentId, DepartmentName, and DepartmentDescription as shown below.

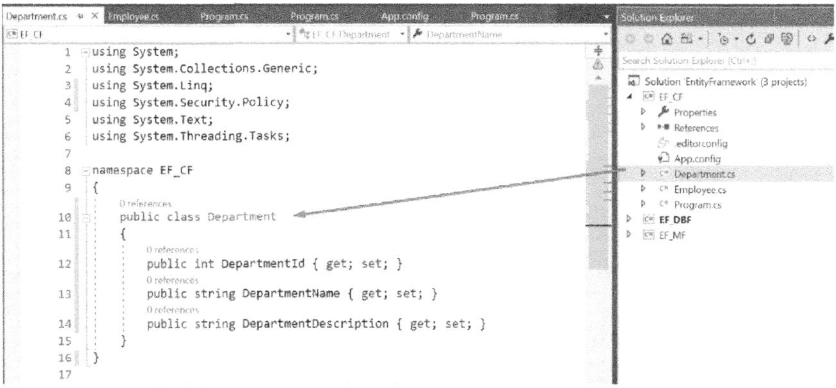

4. Since an employee belongs to one department, each employee would have a related department to it, so add a new property named DepartmentId to the Employee class.

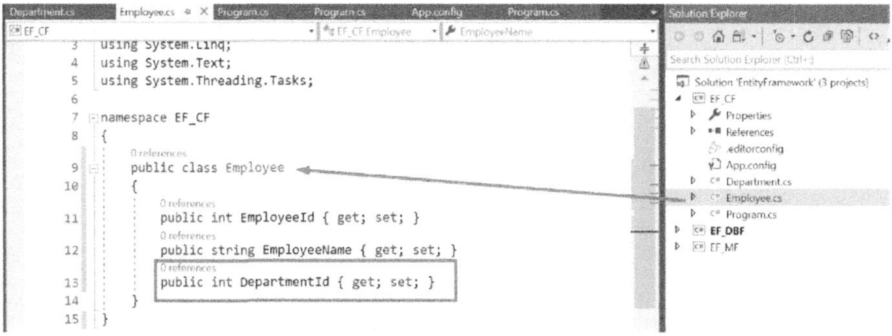

5. Now, time to add EntityFramework to our project. Open package manager console, select default project as your current console application and install Entity Framework. We already

did this a couple of time before, so it won't be a problem now on how to install it.

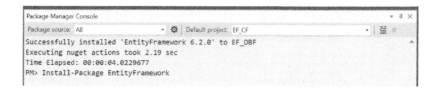

6. Since we are doing everything from scratch. We need our DbContext class as well. In model first and database first, we got the DB context class generated. But, in this case, we would need to create it manually. Add a new class named CodeFirstContext to the project which inherits from DbContext class of namespace System.Data.Entity as shown in the following image. Now add two DbSet properties named Employees and Departments as shown in the following image.

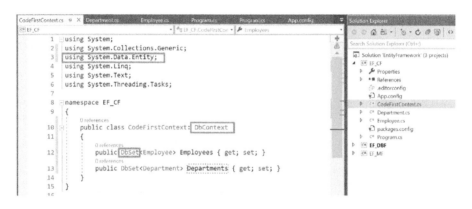

The final code may look like,

```
using System;
using System.Collections.Generic;
using System.Data.Entity;
using System.Linq;
using System.Text;
using System.Threading.Tasks;

namespace EF_CF {
    public class CodeFirstContext: DbContext {
        public DbSet<Employee> Employees { get; set;
}
```

```
        public DbSet<Department> Departments { get;
set; }
      }
}
```

DbSet

DbContext

Both DbContext and DbSet are our superheroes, in creating and dealing with database operations, and make us far abstracted, providing ease of use to us.

When we are working with DbContext, we are in real working with entity sets. DbSet represents a typed entity set that is used to perform create, read, update, and delete operations. We are not creating DbSet objects and using them independently. DbSet can be only used with DbContext.

7. Let's try to make our implementation a more abstract and instead of accessing dbContext directly from the controller, let's abstract it in a class named DataAccessHelper. This class will act as a helper class for all our database operations. So, add a new class named DataAccessHelper to the project.

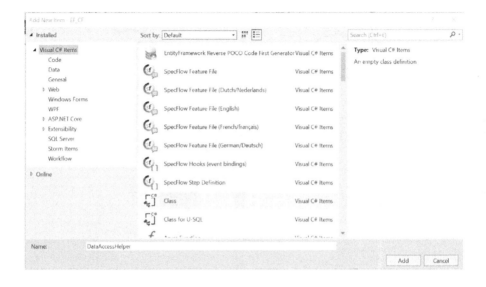

8. Create a read-only instance of the DB context class and add few
    methods like FetchEmployees() to get employees details,
    FetchDepartments() to fetch department details. One method
    each to add employee and add a department. You can add
    more methods at your will like the update and delete
    operations. For now, we'll stick to these four methods.

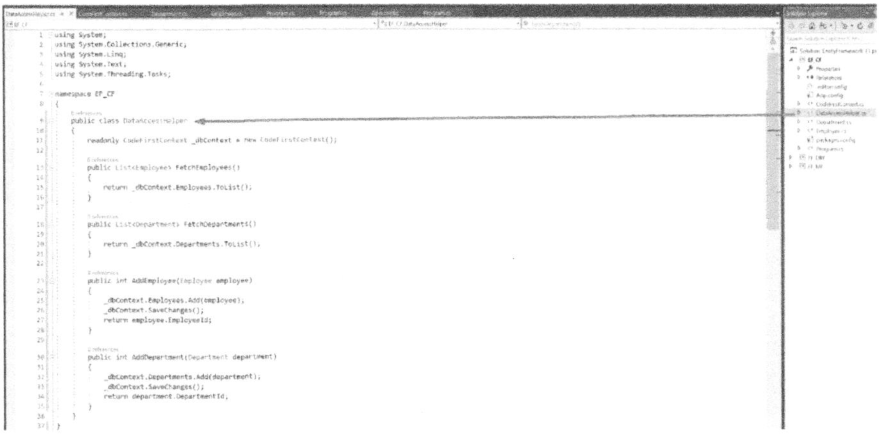

The code may look like as shown below,

```csharp
using System;
using System.Collections.Generic;
using System.Linq;
using System.Text;
using System.Threading.Tasks;

namespace EF_CF
{
    public class DataAccessHelper
    {
```

```csharp
        readonly CodeFirstContext _dbContext = new
CodeFirstContext();

        public List<Employee> FetchEmployees() {
            return _dbContext.Employees.ToList();
        }

        public List<Department> FetchDepartments() {
            return _dbContext.Departments.ToList();
        }

        public int AddEmployee(Employee employee) {
            _dbContext.Employees.Add(employee);
            _dbContext.SaveChanges();
            return employee.EmployeeId;
        }

        public int AddDepartment(Department
department) {
            _dbContext.Departments.Add(department);
            _dbContext.SaveChanges();
            return department.DepartmentId;
        }
    }
}
```

9. Let's add the concept of navigation property now. Navigation properties are those properties of the class through which one can access related entities via the Entity Framework while fetching data. So, while fetching Employee data we may need to fetch the details of its related Departments and while fetching Department data we may need to fetch the details of associated employees with that. Navigation properties are added as virtual properties in the entity. So, in Employee class, add a property for Departments returning a single Department entity and make it virtual. Similarly, in Department class, add a property named Employees returning the collection of Employee entity and make that virtual too.

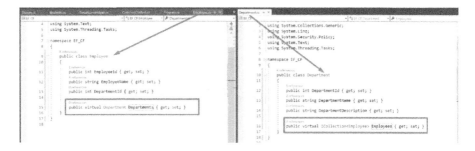

Following is the code for the Employee and the Department model,

Employee

```
using System;
using System.Collections.Generic;
using System.Linq;
using System.Text;
using System.Threading.Tasks;

namespace EF_CF
```

```
{
    public class Employee
    {
        public int EmployeeId { get; set; }
        public string EmployeeName { get; set; }
        public int DepartmentId { get; set; }
        public virtual Department Departments { get;
set; }
    }
}
```

Department

```
using System;
using System.Collections.Generic;
using System.Linq;
using System.Security.Policy;
using System.Text;
using System.Threading.Tasks;

namespace EF_CF
{
    public class Department
    {
        public int DepartmentId { get; set; }
        public string DepartmentName { get; set; }
        public string DepartmentDescription { get;
set; }
        public virtual ICollection<Employee>
Employees { get; set;  }
    }
}
```

10. Let's write some code to perform database operations with our code. So, in the Main() method of Program.cs class add the following sample test code,

```
using System;
using System.Collections.Generic;
using System.Linq;
using System.Text;
using System.Threading.Tasks;

namespace EF_CF
{
    class Program
    {
        static void Main(string[] args)
        {
            Department department = new Department
            {
                DepartmentName = "Technology",
                Employees = new List<Employee>
                {
                    new Employee() {EmployeeName =
"Jack"},
                    new Employee() {EmployeeName =
"Kim"},
                    new Employee() {EmployeeName =
"Shen"}
                }
            };
            DataAccessHelper dbHelper = new
DataAccessHelper();
            dbHelper.AddDepartment(department);
            var addedDepartment =
dbHelper.FetchDepartments().FirstOrDefault();
```

```
if (addedDepartment != null)
{
    Console.WriteLine("Department Name
is: " + addedDepartment.DepartmentName +
Environment.NewLine);
    Console.WriteLine("Department
Employees are: " + Environment.NewLine);

    foreach (var addedDepartmentEmployee
in addedDepartment.Employees)
    {

Console.WriteLine(addedDepartmentEmployee.EmployeeNa
me + Environment.NewLine);
    }

    Console.ReadLine();
    }
        }
    }
}
```

In the above code of Main() method, we are trying to create an object of Department class and add a list of Employees to the Employees property of that class. Create an instance of the dbHelper class and invoke the method AddDepartment, passing the department entity object to that method to add the new department.

Just after adding the department, we are fetching the newly added department and just to make sure that the department and its related employees got added successfully to the database. So, we'll fetch the departments and on the console, print the department name and its related employees. But how will all this be done, we do not have a database yet ☹

11. Not to worry, let's see how we can make sure that we get the DB created from our code. First like we saw earlier, our context class name should be the same as our connection string name or vice versa. So, add a connection string having the same name as DB context class in the App.config file as shown below.

```xml
<?xml version="1.0" encoding="utf-8"?>
<configuration>
  <configSections>
    <!-- For more information on Entity Framework configuration, visit http://go.microsoft.com/fwlink/?LinkID=237468 -->
    <section name="entityFramework" type="System.Data.Entity.Internal.ConfigFile.EntityFrameworkSection, EntityFramework, Version=6.0.0.0, Culture=neutr
  </configSections>
  <startup>
    <supportedRuntime version="v4.0" sku=".NETFramework,Version=v4.6" />
  </startup>
  <connectionStrings>
    <add name="CodeFirstContext"
      connectionString="Server=localhost;Database=codefirstdb;integrated security=true;"
      providerName="System.Data.SqlClient" />
  </connectionStrings>
  <entityFramework>
    <defaultConnectionFactory type="System.Data.Entity.Infrastructure.LocalDbConnectionFactory, EntityFramework">
      <parameters>
        <parameter value="mssqllocaldb" />
      </parameters>
    </defaultConnectionFactory>
    <providers>
      <provider invariantName="System.Data.SqlClient" type="System.Data.Entity.SqlServer.SqlProviderServices, EntityFramework.SqlServer" />
    </providers>
  </entityFramework>
</configuration>
```

Job done. Entity Framework will take care of rest of the pending work of creating a database. We just run the application and now, DB context class is first used to perform a DB operation, we get our database created.

12. Put a breakpoint on the main method and run the application.

```csharp
using System.Text;
using System.Threading.Tasks;

namespace EF_CF
{
    class Program
    {
        static void Main(string[] args)
        {
            Department department = new Department
            {
                DepartmentName = "Technology",
                Employees = new List<Employee>
                {
                    new Employee() {EmployeeName = "Jack"},
                    new Employee() {EmployeeName = "Kim"},
                    new Employee() {EmployeeName = "Shen"}
                }
            };
            DataAccessHelper dbHelper = new DataAccessHelper();
            dbHelper.AddDepartment(department);
            var addedDepartment = dbHelper.FetchDepartments().FirstOrDefault();
            if (addedDepartment != null)
            {
                Console.WriteLine("Department Name is: " + addedDepartment.DepartmentName + Environment.NewLine);
                Console.WriteLine("Department Employees are: " + Environment.NewLine);

                foreach (var addedDepartmentEmployee in addedDepartment.Employees)
                {
                    Console.WriteLine(addedDepartmentEmployee.EmployeeName + Environment.NewLine);
                }

                Console.ReadLine();
            }
        }
    }
}
```

13. As soon as the line where we write the code to AddDepartment gets executed, our database is created.

```
namespace EF_CF
{
    0 references
    class Program
    {
        0 references
        static void Main(string[] args)   args = {string[0]}
        {
            Department department = new Department   department = {Department}
            {
                DepartmentName = "Technology",
                Employees = new List<Employee>
                {
                    new Employee() {EmployeeName = "Jack"},
                    new Employee() {EmployeeName = "Kim"},
                    new Employee() {EmployeeName = "Shen"}
                }
            };
            DataAccessHelper dbHelper = new DataAccessHelper();   dbHelper = {DataAccessHelper}
            dbHelper.AddDepartment(department);   DataAccessHelper.AddDepartment() = 1   ──────── Creates DB
            var addedDepartment = dbHelper.FetchDepartments().FirstOrDefault();   addedDepartment = null   dbHelper = {DataAccessHelper}
            if (addedDepartment != null)
            {
                Console.WriteLine("Department Name is: " + addedDepartment.DepartmentName + Environment.NewLine);
                Console.WriteLine("Department Employees are: " + Environment.NewLine);

                foreach (var addedDepartmentEmployee in addedDepartment.Employees)
                {
                    Console.WriteLine(addedDepartmentEmployee.EmployeeName + Environment.NewLine);
                }

                Console.ReadLine();
            }
        }
    }
}
```

©2018 Akhil Mittal (www.codeteddy.com)

14. Go to the database server and see we got the database created
with the same name that we supplied in the connection string.
We have Departments and Employees table and a table named
__MigrationHistory to track the history of code first migrations
performed on this database.

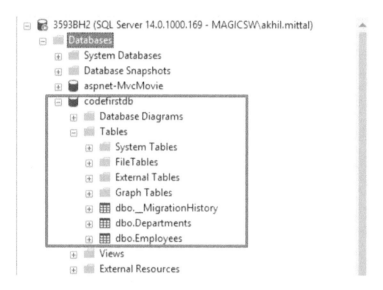

We see that we also got one Department added in the database having
the name "Technology" that we used in the code.

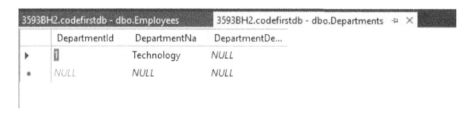

And, got our employee's table filled with three rows having three employees with department id 1 i.e. the id of the newly added department. And so, our code first approach worked as well ▨

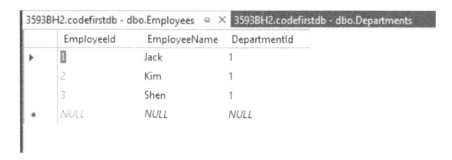

15. You can proceed to press F5, to run the application and when console window appears we see the details of the department and added employees in that window, so our fetch operations also work fine.

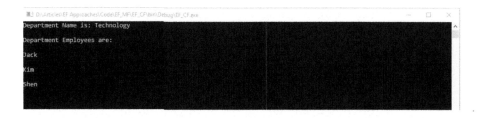

Though we covered all the approaches of the Entity Framework. I would like to show the code first migrations as well now to make you understand how to code first migrations work with Entity Framework. Before that, we need to know what is the requirement of migrations and what is the benefit of having migrations while working with code first approach.

Code First Options

The Entity Framework code first approach provides us with three approaches while creating the database.

CreateDatabaseIfNotExists

It is the default option provided as an initializer class for code first approach. This option helps us create a database only if there is no existing database and so any accidental dropping of the database could be avoided via this option.

DropCreateDatabaseWhenModelChanges

This initializer class keeps an eye on the underlying model and if the model changes, it drops the existing database and re-creates a new one. It is useful when the application is not live and the development and testing phase is going on.

DropCreateDatabaseAlways

This option as the name says always drops and creates a database whenever you run the application. It is most useful in testing when you are testing with the new set of data every time.

Code First Migrations

Imagine a scenario where you want to add a new model/entity and you do not want the existing database to get deleted or changed when you update the database with the newly added model class. Code first migrations here help you to update the existing database with your newly added model classes and your existing database remains intact with the existing data. So, the data and the schema won't be created again.

Code First Migrations in Action

Let's see how we can work with code first migrations step by step like we did for other approaches.

1. Add a new console application named EF_CF_Migrations.

2. Add the Department model with properties DepartmentId, DepartmentName and DepartmentDescription. Add a virtual property as a navigation property called Employees because a department can have multiple employees.

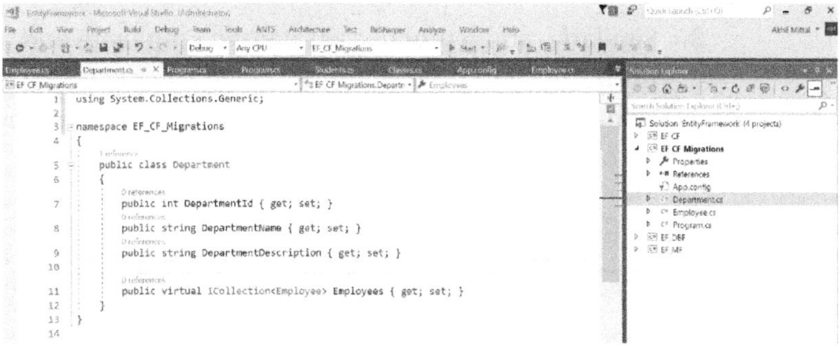

using System.Collections.Generic;
namespace EF_CF_Migrations
{
public class Department
{
public int DepartmentId { get; set; }
public string DepartmentName { get; set; }
public string DepartmentDescription { get; set; }
public virtual ICollection<Employee> Employees { get; set; }
}
}
Solution Explorer
Solution EntityFramework (4 projects)
EF CF
EF CF Migrations
Properties
References
App.config
Department.cs
Employee.cs
Program.cs
EF DBF
EF MF

3. Similarly, add a model class named Employee and add three
    properties as EmployeeId, EmployeeName, DepartmentId, and
    Departments as a navigation property as an employee may be
    associated with any department.

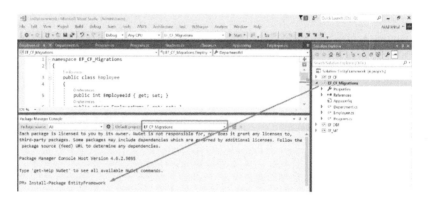

4. Install Entity Framework from the package manager console as
    shown in the following image.

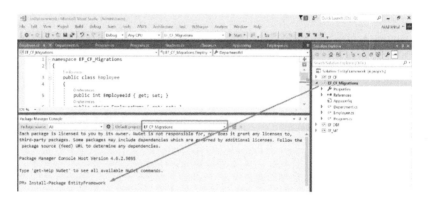

5. Add a context class deriving from DbContext class and add Employee and Department class as a DbSet property in the class.

6. Now, execute command named "Enable-Migrations" but before that select the default project as your newly added project. The command has to be executed using the package manager console.

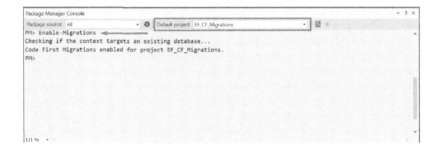

7. Once the command is executed, you'll get a folder in your application named "Migrations" and by default, a class named Configuration would be added that holds your initial configurations and all other configurations you want to have with code first approach. You can configure the settings in the constructor of this class. This class derives from DbMigrationsConfigurations which has a virtual method Seed in the base class. We can override the method in our derived class to add some seed data to our database when it gets created.

8. The Seed method takes the context as a parameter. Context is the instance of our CodeFirstContext class. Now add sample data to the context for e.g. as shown below, I am adding one department named Technology with three sample employees and one additional employee separately to the context. The class will look like the code below.

```csharp
using System.Collections.Generic;

namespace EF_CF_Migrations.Migrations
{
    using System;
    using System.Data.Entity;
    using System.Data.Entity.Migrations;
    using System.Linq;

    internal sealed class Configuration :
DbMigrationsConfiguration<EF_CF_Migrations.CodeFirst
Context>
    {
        public Configuration()
        {
            AutomaticMigrationsEnabled = false;
        }

        protected override void
Seed(EF_CF_Migrations.CodeFirstContext context)
        {
            Department department = new Department
            {
                DepartmentName = "Technology",
                Employees = new List<Employee>
                {
```

```
                    new Employee() {EmployeeName =
"Jack"},
                    new Employee() {EmployeeName =
"Kim"},
                    new Employee() {EmployeeName =
"Shen"}
            }
        };

        Employee employee = new Employee
        {
            EmployeeName = "Akhil Mittal",
            DepartmentId = 1
        };


context.Departments.AddOrUpdate(department);
        context.Employees.AddOrUpdate(employee);
        }
    }
}
```

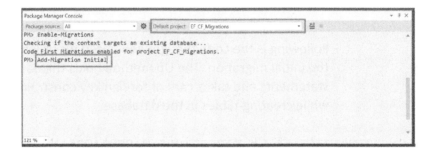

9. Now execute one more command that says "Add-Migration Initial" on package manager console. This command, when executed, creates one more file under the Migrations folder.

The name of the file comprises of the date-time stamp and is appended with the keyword "_Initial". This class derives from DbMigration class that has a virtual Up() method. The command overrides this method in the generated class and adds statements to create the database tables when our code will execute. Similarly, the Down() method is the opposite of the Up() method.

Following is the code that got generated for us when we added the initial migration. The Up method holds the database statements and takes care of foreign key constraints as well while creating tables in the database.

```
namespace EF_CF_Migrations.Migrations
{
    using System;
    using System.Data.Entity.Migrations;

    public partial class Initial : DbMigration
    {
        public override void Up()
        {
            CreateTable(
```

```
                "dbo.Departments",
                c => new
                    {
                        DepartmentId =
c.Int(nullable: false, identity: true),
                        DepartmentName = c.String(),
                        DepartmentDescription =
c.String(),
                    })
                .PrimaryKey(t => t.DepartmentId);

            CreateTable(
                "dbo.Employees",
                c => new
                    {
                        EmployeeId = c.Int(nullable:
false, identity: true),
                        EmployeeName = c.String(),
                        DepartmentId =
c.Int(nullable: false),
                    })
                .PrimaryKey(t => t.EmployeeId)
                .ForeignKey("dbo.Departments", t =>
t.DepartmentId, cascadeDelete: true)
                .Index(t => t.DepartmentId);

        }

        public override void Down()
        {
            DropForeignKey("dbo.Employees",
"DepartmentId", "dbo.Departments");
            DropIndex("dbo.Employees", new[] {
"DepartmentId" });
```

```
        DropTable("dbo.Employees");
        DropTable("dbo.Departments");
    }
  }
}
```

10. There still is a gap that needs to be bridged before we proceed. We'll need to have a connection string with the same name as of our context class in our App.config. So, open the App.config file of the project and add the connection string as needed with the server and database name details.

11. The last step of migrations is to execute a command that says "Update-Database".

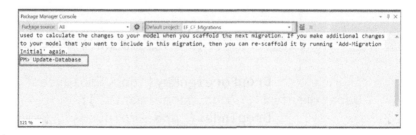

This command, when executed on package manager console, applies all the migrations we have under the Migrations folder and runs the seed method of Configuration class.

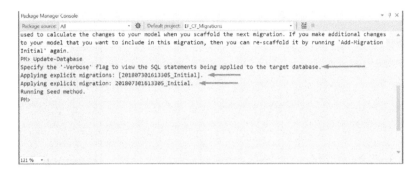

12. Now, go to the database to check if we got our tables created or not with the sample data that we provided in seed method. In the image below, we see the Departments table having the sample department that we added in seed method to context as Department model.

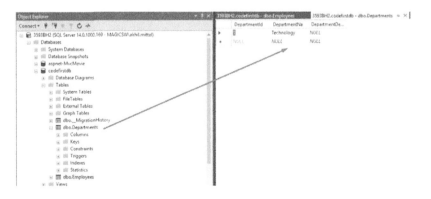

In the Employees table, we have all the employees associated with that department and one additional employee as well that we added via seed method.

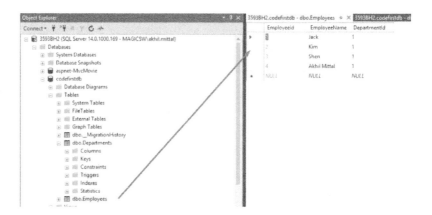

13. Let's add some code to our program.cs class to check if the database operations are working fine or not. So, create an instance of CodeFirstContext and add one more sample department with sample employees and save the changes.

```
class Program
{
    0 references
    static void Main(string[] args)
    {
        CodeFirstContext context =new CodeFirstContext();

        Department department = new Department
        {
            DepartmentName = "Management",
            Employees = new List<Employee>
            {
                new Employee() {EmployeeName = "Hui"},
                new Employee() {EmployeeName = "Dui"},
                new Employee() {EmployeeName = "Lui"}
            }
        };
        context.Departments.Add(department);
        context.SaveChanges();
    }
}
```

Following is the code.

```
using System;
using System.Collections.Generic;
using System.Linq;
using System.Text;
using System.Threading.Tasks;

namespace EF_CF_Migrations {
    class Program        {
        static void Main(string[] args)
        {
            CodeFirstContext context =new
CodeFirstContext();

            Department department = new Department
            {
                DepartmentName = "Management",
                Employees = new List<Employee>
                {
                    new Employee() {EmployeeName =
"Hui"},
                    new Employee() {EmployeeName =
"Dui"},
                    new Employee() {EmployeeName =
"Lui"}
                }
            };
            context.Departments.Add(department);
            context.SaveChanges();
        }
    }
}
```

14. Run the code by pressing F5 and then go to the database to check if the records for department and Employees associated with it got inserted or not. We see in the following image while selecting top records from Departments table, we get one additional department that we just created.

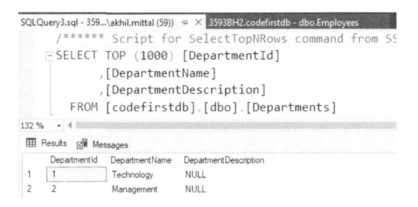

Similarly, we get added Employees for the newly added department as shown in the following image.

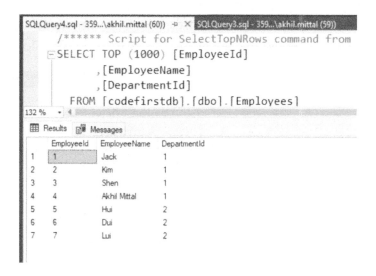

MigrationHistory Table

This is the most important part of code first migrations. We see that along with our entity tables we got an additional table named __MigrationHistory. This table takes responsibility to hold all the migrations history that we add from code. For e.g. check the row that it got initially. The MigrationId column of the first row contains the value that is the same as the name of the file that got created when we added migrations in our code. It contains the hash and every time we add or modify something in the model and run update migrations command, it checks the history in the database and compares with the existing files of migrations that we have in our Migrations folder. If the file is new, it executes that file only and not the old ones. This helps us to track database changes in the more organized way. One can also revert back to a particular migration from code by supplying the migration id of that migration. Migration id is nothing but the name of the migration file and the same that got stored in the __MigrationHistory table as the column value. The following two images show that the column value in the MigrationHistory table and the file name in the code for migration is similar.

In case, you add a new migration, a new file would be created with a unique name having date-time stamp and when you run update migration, a new row will be inserted into the __MigrationHistory table for the same having same column value as the name of the newly added file.

Querying in Entity Framework

Querying means writing the query to perform database operations and the queries should be converted into native SQL queries to perform operations. EF provides the querying options where a developer does not really need to know SQL or database languages. Querying in Entity Framework could be performed via three methods as follows.

1. LINQ to Entities (L2E)
2. Entity SQL
3. Native SQL

LINQ to SQL

Developers can fully utilize their LINQ skills if they chose to write queries in L2E. It allows the queries to be written directly to the entities or domain classes for database operations like create, update, delete or read. In the sample applications created in previous sections, L2E was frequently used to query the data or for other db operations. For e.g. to fetch the detail of a department following is the query that could be written.

```
var query = context.Departments.where(d => d.Department
Name == "Technology")
                        .FirstOrDefault<Department>();
```

Entity SQL

Entity SQL could be another way but a bit tricky than LINQ to Entity. Object Service layer of Entity Framework architecture takes care of this query to be converted to database specific query to fetch or save data.

For e.g. the query could be following that, in turn, would be used by object context to return object query.

```
string query = "SELECT VALUE dep FROM context.Departmen
ts " +

                    "AS dep WHERE dep.DepartmentName ==
'Technology'";


var objectContext = (context as IObjectContextAdapter).
ObjectContext;

ObjectQuery<Department> department = objectContext.Crea
teQuery<Department>(query);

Department fetchedDep = department.FirstOrDefault<Depar
tment>();
```

Native SQL

Entity framework does not restrict the developers to completely cut off from the database and is equally friendly for the developers who are not very good at LINQ and good at SQL. One can write native SQL queries as well using Entity Framework, without worrying about connections and commands.

```
var department = ctx.Departments.SqlQuery("Select * fro
m Department where DepartmentName='Technology'").FirstO
rDefault<Department>();
```

Similarly, one can invoke stored procedures or functions using this native SQL approach.

Loadings in Entity Framework

Entity Framework has an amazing feature to load the related data. To clarify this more, EF gives the possibilities to load the data for the related entity while fetching the data for an entity. For e.g., if there are two tables which are related via foreign key references, EF while creating the model/entity classes for those adds a virtual navigation property in the entities so that when data for one entity is fetched, the data for another related entity could be fetched via that navigation property. Entity Framework offers three ways which could be used to fetch related data based on the need. It also provides the option to disable loading related data. Subjective to the need one can enable or disable this feature or can use any of the three approaches to load the related data. By default, if the data of an entity is loaded its related tables data will also be loaded as a query and can only be executed on the database when used. This feature is called Lazy Loading. Following are the three approaches through which we can load related table data or related data for entities.

1. Lazy Loading
2. Eager Loading
3. Explicit Loading

Lazy Loading

EF gives the flexibility to delay the loading of related data until the same is requested. The data for the related entity would be loaded in the form of query i.e. actual data is not loaded but the query is prepared as the part of the entity to load the related data. Once that query is used or requested, then the actual database query is executed, and the data is fetched. It is delayed loading or also called on-demand loading and when used wisely could result in very optimized code and improve application performance. This loading if not used wisely could result in disaster and may end up fetching related data that is not needed before we need that and could have a huge performance impact especially if the related tables have a lot of data. An example of lazy loading could be that when we fetch a department from the database, the related students for that department should also load.

```
//Loading Departments only

IList<Department> departments = context.Departments
.ToList<Department>();

Department department = departments [0];

//Loads Employees for particular Department only

Employee employee = department.Employees;
```

One can easily disable lazy loading for complete application and all the entities by setting its configuration property in the constructor of applications DbContext class.

```
this.Configuration.LazyLoadingEnabled = false;
```

If it must be disabled for an entity property, then just do not make the property virtual and it will not lazily load the related data.

Eager Loading

Eager loading is opposite of Lazy loading. Eager loading when used loads the data of related entities as part of the single query and no other SQL query is executed to fetch related data. So, no delayed loading but the data is loaded for related entities in the single query in the first attempt. It is used with the help of Include() method. For e.g., if you want to load the data of related employees of the department at the time of loading departments, you can use Eager loading.

```
var department = context.Departments.Include(dep => dep
.Employees)
                              .Where(dep => dep.Departmen
tName == "Management")
                              .FirstOrDefault<Department>
();
```

You can use, multiple includes to include data from multiple entities as well.

Explicit Loading

It is a feature where if lazy loading is disabled, one can load the related entities via explicit calls. This feature makes use of Load() method to load the related entities lazily even when lazy loading is globally disabled at context level.

```
var department = context.Departments
                         .Where(dep => dep.DepartmentNam
e == "Management")
```

```
                        .FirstOrDefault<Department>();
    context.Entry(department).Reference(dep => dep.Empl
oyees).Load();
```

In the mentioned example **context.Entry(department).Reference(dep => dep.Employees).Load();** loads related Employees for the fetched department even if lazy loading is disabled.

Code First Migrations in ASP.NET Web API 2.0

In this section, we'll learn how to perform CRUD operations with ASP.NET Web API2 and Entity Framework. We'll go step by step in a form of tutorial to set up basic Web API project and we'll use code first approach of Entity Framework to generate database and perform CRUD operations. We'll not create a client for this application but rather use Postman i.e. the tool to test REST endpoints.

Web API

I completely agree with the following excerpt from Microsoft documents
"HTTP is not just for serving up web pages. HTTP is also a powerful platform for building APIs that expose services and data. HTTP is simple, flexible, and ubiquitous. Almost any platform that you can think of has an HTTP library, so HTTP services can reach a broad range of clients, including browsers, mobile devices, and traditional desktop applications.ASP.NET Web API is a framework for building web APIs on top of the .NET Framework."

And there is a lot of theory you can read about Web API on MSDN.

Creating a Web API Project

Follow the steps mentioned below with images to create a web API 2 project.

1. I am using Visual Studio 2017 for this tutorial. Open the Visual Studio and add a new project.

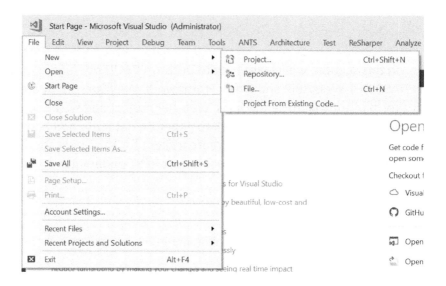

2. Choose the "Web" option in installed templates and choose "ASP.NET Web Application (.NET Framework)". Change the name of the solution and project for e.g. Project name could be "StudentManagement" and Solution name could be "WebAPI2WithEF". Choose the framework as .net Framework 4.6. Click OK.

3. When you click OK, you'll be prompted to choose the type of ASP.NET Web Application. Choose Web API and click OK.

4. Once you click OK, you'll have default basic Web API project with required NuGet packages, files and folders with Views and Controllers to run the application.

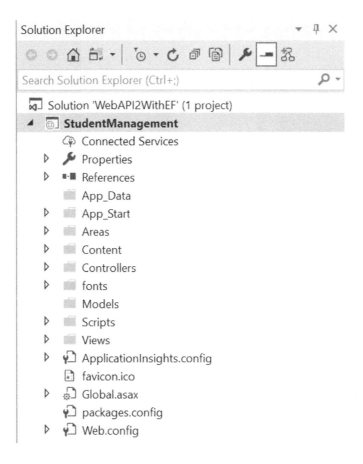

Creating the model

We'll create a model class that will act as an entity for Student on which we need to perform database operations. We'll keep it simple just for the sake of understanding on how it works. You could create multiple model classes and even can have a relationship between those.

1. Right-click Models folder and add a new class. Name the class as "Student"

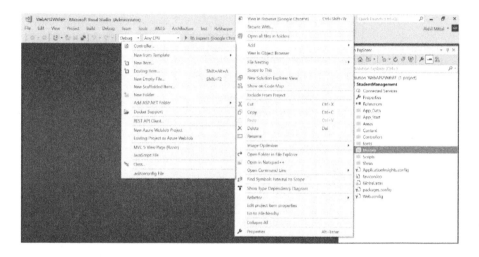

2. Make the class public and add two properties to the class i.e. Id and Name. Id will serve as a primary key for this entity.

```
1  using System;
2  using System.Collections.Generic;
3  using System.Linq;
4  using System.Web;
5
6  namespace StudentManagement.Models
7  {
       12 references
8      public class Student
9      {
           4 references
10         public int Id { get; set; }
           3 references
11         public string Name { get; set; }
12     }
13 }
```

```
using System;
using System.Collections.Generic;
using System.Linq;
using System.Web;

namespace StudentManagement.Models
{
    public class Student
    {
        public int Id { get; set; }
        public string Name { get; set; }
    }
}
```

3. Rebuild the solution.

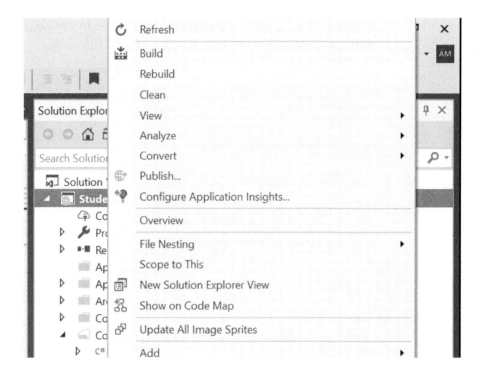

Adding the API Controller

Let's add a controller that will contain the database operations for create, update, read and delete over our model class.

1. Right click the controller folder and add choose the option to add a new controller class.

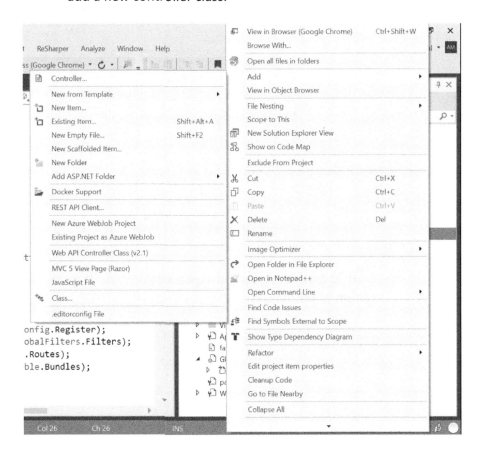

2. In the next prompt, choose the option to create a Web API 2 Controller with actions, using Entity Framework. Click on Add button.

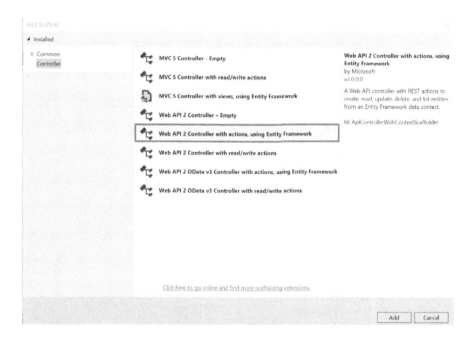

3. Next, choose the model we created i.e. Student model in the option of Model class.

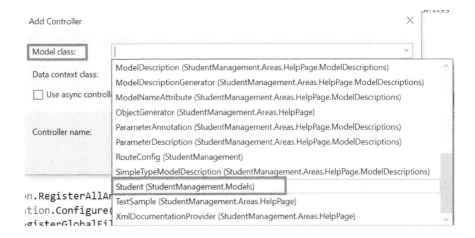

4. Since we do not have data context for our application, click on the + button close to Data context class option dropdown, and provide the name "StudentManagementContext" in the text box shown and click Add.

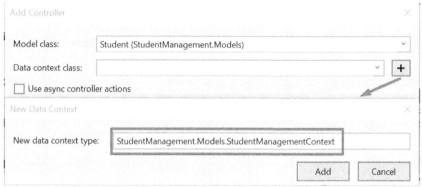

5. The name of the controller should be "StudentsController". Click Add to finish.

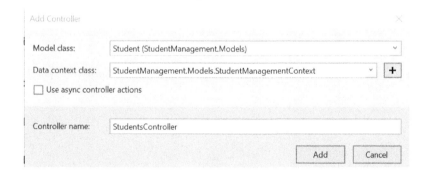

6. Once you click Add to finish, it will try to create a scaffolding template of the controller with all read/write actions using Entity Framework and our model class. This will also add the reference to Entity Framework and related NuGet packages because it is smart enough to understand that we want our controller to have database operations using Entity Framework as we mentioned the same in the second step on adding a controller. Creating scaffolding template may take a while.

Microsoft Visual Studio

Scaffolding...

7. Once the template is generated, you can see the controller class added to the Controller folder in the Web API project. This controller class derives from ApiController class and has all the methods that may be needed for performing a database operation on the student entity. If we check the method names, those are prefixed with the name of the verb for which the method is intended to perform an action. That is the way the end request is mapped to the actions. If you do not want your actions to be prefixed with the HTTP verbs, you can decorate your methods with HTTP verb attributes, placing the attribute over the method or applying attribute routing over the actions. We'll not discuss those in detail and will stick to this implementation.

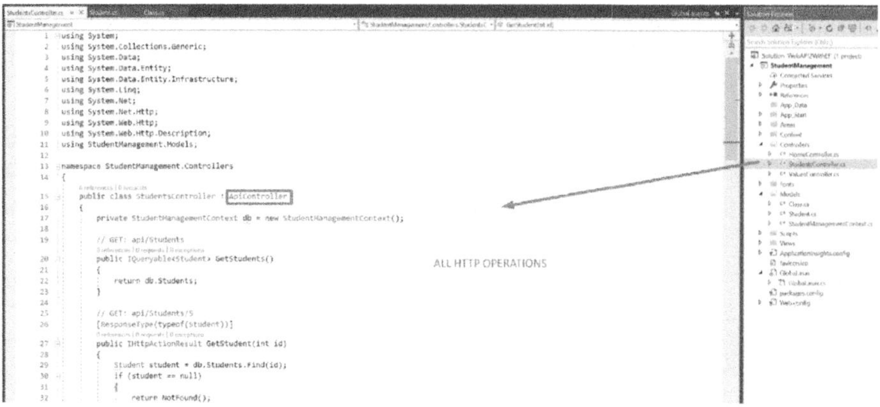

ALL HTTP OPERATIONS

Controller class code:

```csharp
using System;
using System.Collections.Generic;
using System.Data;
using System.Data.Entity;
using System.Data.Entity.Infrastructure;
using System.Linq;
using System.Net;
using System.Net.Http;
using System.Web.Http;
using System.Web.Http.Description;
using StudentManagement.Models;

namespace StudentManagement.Controllers
{
    public class StudentsController : ApiController
    {
        private StudentManagementContext db = new StudentManagementContext();

        // GET: api/Students
        public IQueryable<Student> GetStudents()
        {
            return db.Students;
        }

        // GET: api/Students/5
        [ResponseType(typeof(Student))]
        public IHttpActionResult GetStudent(int id)
        {
            Student student = db.Students.Find(id);
            if (student == null)
            {
```

```
            return NotFound();
        }

        return Ok(student);
    }

    // PUT: api/Students/5
    [ResponseType(typeof(void))]
    public IHttpActionResult PutStudent(int id,
Student student)
    {
        if (!ModelState.IsValid)
        {
            return BadRequest(ModelState);
        }

        if (id != student.Id)
        {
            return BadRequest();
        }

        db.Entry(student).State =
EntityState.Modified;

        try
        {
            db.SaveChanges();
        }
        catch (DbUpdateConcurrencyException)
        {
            if (!StudentExists(id))
            {
                return NotFound();
            }
```

```
                else
                {
                    throw;
                }
            }

            return
StatusCode(HttpStatusCode.NoContent);
        }

        // POST: api/Students
        [ResponseType(typeof(Student))]
        public IHttpActionResult PostStudent(Student
student)
        {
            if (!ModelState.IsValid)
            {
                return BadRequest(ModelState);
            }

            db.Students.Add(student);
            db.SaveChanges();

            return CreatedAtRoute("DefaultApi", new
{ id = student.Id }, student);
        }

        // DELETE: api/Students/5
        [ResponseType(typeof(Student))]
        public IHttpActionResult DeleteStudent(int
id)
        {
            Student student = db.Students.Find(id);
            if (student == null)
```

```csharp
            {
                return NotFound();
            }

            db.Students.Remove(student);
            db.SaveChanges();

            return Ok(student);
        }

        protected override void Dispose(bool
disposing)
        {
            if (disposing)
            {
                db.Dispose();
            }
            base.Dispose(disposing);
        }

        private bool StudentExists(int id)
        {
            return db.Students.Count(e => e.Id ==
id) > 0;
        }
    }
}
```

Entity Framework Code First Migrations

Imagine a scenario where you want to add a new model/entity and you do not want the existing database to get deleted or changed when you update the database with the newly added model class. Code first migrations here help you to update the existing database with your newly added model classes and your existing database remains intact with the existing data. So, the data and the schema won't be created again. It is a code first approach and we'll see how we can enable this in our application step by step.

1. Open Package Manager Console and select the default project as your WebAPI project. Type the command **Enable-Migrations** and press enter.

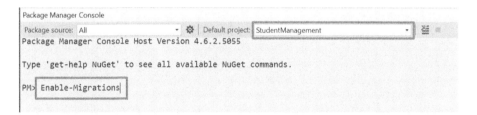

2. Once the command is executed, it does some changes to our solution. As a part of adding migrations, it creates a Migrations folder and adds a class file named **"Configuration.cs"**. This class is derived from DbMigrationsConfiguration class. This class contains a Seed method having the parameter as the context class that we got generated in the Models folder. Seed is an overridden method that means it contains a virtual method in a base class and a class driven from DbMigrationsConfiguration can override that and add custom functionality. We can utilize the Seed method to provide seed data or master data to the

database if we want that when our database is created there should be some data in a few tables.

DbMigrationsConfiguration class:

```
Assembly EntityFramework, Version=6.0.0.0, Culture=neutral, PublicKeyT

using ...

namespace System.Data.Entity.Migrations
{
    public class DbMigrationsConfiguration<TContext> : DbMigrations
    {
        public DbMigrationsConfiguration();

        public override bool Equals(object obj);
        public override int GetHashCode();
        public Type GetType();
        public override string ToString();
        protected object MemberwiseClone();
        protected virtual void Seed(TContext context);
    }
}
```

3. Let's utilize this Seed method and add a few students in the Students model. I am adding three students named Allen, Kim, and Jane.

```
0 references
protected override void Seed(StudentManagement.Models.StudentManagementContext context)
{
    context.Students.AddOrUpdate(p => p.Id,
        new Student { Name = "Allen" },
        new Student { Name = "Kim" },
        new Student { Name = "Jane" }
    );

}
```

Configuration Class:

```
using StudentManagement.Models;

namespace StudentManagement.Migrations
{
    using System;
    using System.Data.Entity;
    using System.Data.Entity.Migrations;
    using System.Linq;

    internal sealed class Configuration :
DbMigrationsConfiguration<StudentManagement.Models.S
tudentManagementContext>
    {
        public Configuration()
        {
            AutomaticMigrationsEnabled = false;
        }

        protected override void
Seed(StudentManagement.Models.StudentManagementConte
xt context)
        {
            context.Students.AddOrUpdate(p => p.Id,
                new Student { Name = "Allen" },
                new Student { Name = "Kim" },
                new Student { Name = "Jane" }
            );

        }
    }
}
```

4. The context parameter is the instance of our context class that got generated while we were adding a controller. We provided the name as StudentManagementContext. This class derives from DbContext class. This context class takes care of DB schema and the DbSet properties of this class are basically the tables that we'll have when our database will be created. It added Students as a DbSet property that returns our Student model/entity and would be directly mapped to the table that will be generated in the database.

5. Next step is to execute the command named "Add-Migrations". In the package manager console execute this command with a parameter of your choice that would be the name of our first migration. I call it "Initial". So, the command would be **Add-Migrations Initial**

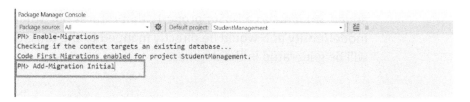

```
Package Manager Console
Package source: All          ▾  ⚙  Default project: StudentManagement          ▾  ⌗
PM> Enable-Migrations
Checking if the context targets an existing database...
Code First Migrations enabled for project StudentManagement.
PM> Add-Migration Initial
```

6. Once the command is executed, it adds a new file with the name "Initial" prefixed with the date time stamp. It prefixes the date time stamp so that it could track the various migrations added during development and segregate between those. Open the file and we see the class named "Initial" deriving from DbMigration class. This class contains two methods that are overridden from DbMigration class i.e. the base class. The method names are Up() and Down(). Up method is executed to add all the initial configuration to the database and contains the create command in LINQ format. This helps to generate tables and all the modifications done over the model. Down command is vice versa of Up command. The code in the file is self-explanatory. The Up command here is having the code that creates the Students table and setting Id as its primary key. All this information is derived from the model and its changes.

```
StudentManagementContext.cs    201808071716385_Initial.cs  ⊕ ×  Configuration.cs    Student.cs    StudentsController.cs
StudentManagement                                                            ▼  StudentManagement.Migrations.I
     1   ☐namespace StudentManagement.Migrations
     2    {
     3   ☐    using System;
     4         using System.Data.Entity.Migrations;
     5
               2 references
     6   ☐    public partial class Initial : DbMigration
     7         {
               0 references
     8   ☐        public override void Up()
     9             {
    10                 CreateTable(
    11                     "dbo.Students",
    12                     c => new
    13                         {
    14                             Id = c.Int(nullable: false, identity: true),
    15                             Name = c.String(),
    16                         })
    17                     .PrimaryKey(t => t.Id);
    18
    19             }
    20
               0 references
    21   ☐        public override void Down()
    22             {
    23                 DropTable("dbo.Students");
    24             }
    25         }
    26    }
    27
```

Initial Migration:

```
namespace StudentManagement.Migrations
{
    using System;
    using System.Data.Entity.Migrations;

    public partial class Initial : DbMigration
    {
        public override void Up()
        {
            CreateTable(
                "dbo.Students",
                c => new
                    {
                        Id = c.Int(nullable: false,
identity: true),
                        Name = c.String(),
                    })
                .PrimaryKey(t => t.Id);

        }

        public override void Down()
        {
            DropTable("dbo.Students");
        }
    }
}
```

7. Again, in the package manager console, run the command
   "Update-Database".

```
Package Manager Console                                                                    ▾
Package source:  All              ▾  ⚙  Default project:  StudentManagement         ▾  ⧉ ▪
The Designer Code for this migration file includes a snapshot of your current Code First model. This snapshot is used
to calculate the changes to your model when you scaffold the next migration. If you make additional changes to your
model that you want to include in this migration, then you can re-scaffold it by running 'Add-Migration Initial' again
PM> Update-Database
```

8. This is the final command that creates the database and respective tables out of our context and model. It executes the Initial migration that we added and then runs the seed method from the configuration class. This command is smart enough to detect which migrations to run. For e.g. it will not run previously executed migrations and all the newly added migrations each time will be taken in to account to be executed to update the database. It maintains this track as the database firstly created contains an additional table named **__MigrationHistory** that keeps track of all the migrations done.

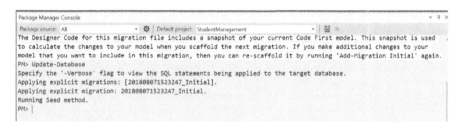

9. On the command is successfully executed, it creates the database in your local database server and adds the corresponding connection string in the Web.Config file. The name of the connection string is the same as the name of our context class and that's how the context class and connection strings are related.

Web.config
Solution Explorer
1 <?xml version="1.0" encoding="utf-8"?>
2 <!--
3 For more information on how to configure your ASP.NET application, please visit
4 https://go.microsoft.com/fwlink/?LinkId=301879
5 -->
6 <configuration>
7 <configSections>
8 <!-- For more information on Entity Framework configuration, visit http://go.microsoft.com/fw
9 <section name="entityFramework" type="System.Data.Entity.Internal.ConfigFile.EntityFrameworkS
10 </configSections>
11 <connectionStrings>
12 <add name="StudentManagementContext"
13 connectionString="Data Source=(localdb)\MSSQLLocalDB;
14 Initial Catalog=StudentManagementContext-20180807203019;
15 Integrated Security=True; MultipleActiveResultSets=True;
16 AttachDbFilename=|DataDirectory|StudentManagementContext-20180807203019.mdf"
17 providerName="System.Data.SqlClient" />
18 </connectionStrings>
19 <appSettings>
20 <add key="webpages:Version" value="3.0.0.0" />
21 <add key="webpages:Enabled" value="false" />
22 <add key="ClientValidationEnabled" value="true" />
23 <add key="UnobtrusiveJavaScriptEnabled" value="true" />
24 </appSettings>
25 <system.web>
References
App_Data
App_Start
Areas
Content
Controllers
HomeController.
StudentsControll
ValuesControlle
fonts
Migrations
Configuration.cs
Models
Class.cs
Student.cs
Scripts
Views
favicon.ico
Global.asax
Global.asax.cs
packages.config
Web.config

Exploring the Generated Database

Let's see what we got in our database when the earlier command got successfully executed.

1. Since we used the local database, we can open it by opening **Server Explorer** from the View tab in Visual Studio itself.

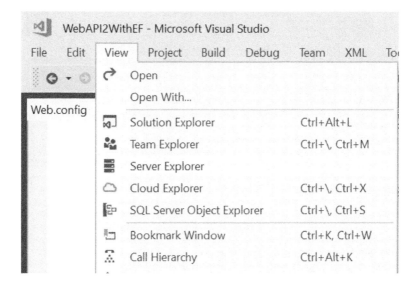

2. Once Server Explorer is shown, we can find the StudentManagementContext database generated and it has two tables named Students and __MigrationHistory. Students table corresponds to our Student model in the code base and __MigrationsHistory table as I mentioned earlier is the auto-generated table that keeps track of the executed migrations.

3. Open the Students table and see the initial data added to the table with three student names that we provided in the Seed method.

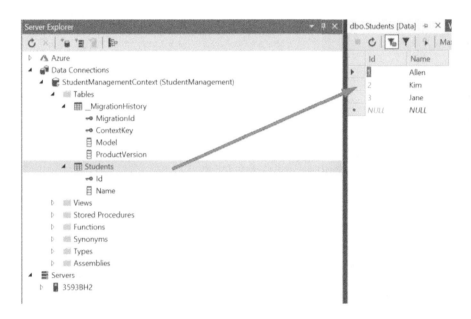

4. Open the __MigrationsHistory table to see the row added for the executed migration with the context key and MigrationId, Migration Id added is the same as the Initial class file name that got generated when we added the migrations through package manager console.

Running the application and Setup Postman

We got our database ready and our application ready. It's time to run the application. Press F5 to run the application from Visual Studio. Once the application is up, you'll see the default home page view launched by the HomeController that was automatically present when we created the WebAPI project.

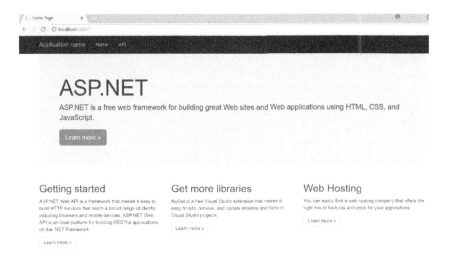

1. Setup Postman. If you already have postman application, directly launch it and if not, search for it on google and install it. The postman will act as a client to our Web API endpoints and will help us in testing the endpoints.

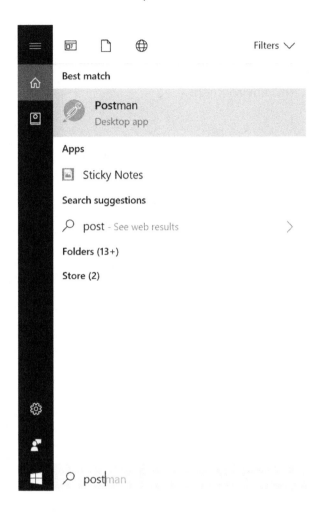

2. Once Postman is opened. You can choose various options from it. I choose the first option to Create basic request. And save the name of the request as TestAPI. We'll do all the tests with this environment.

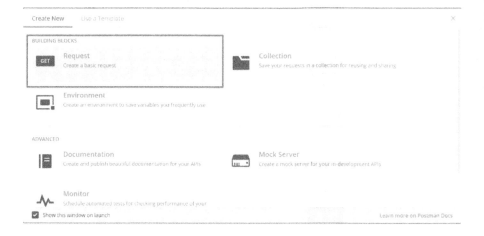

SAVE REQUEST   ✕

Requests in Postman are saved in collections (a group of requests).
Learn more about creating collections

Request name

TestAPI

Request description (Optional)

Test API

Descriptions support Markdown

Select a collection or folder to save to:

🔍 Search for a collection or folder

‹ TestAPI   + Create Folder

Cancel   Save to TestAPI

Endpoints and Database operations

We'll test our endpoints of the API. All the action methods of the StudentsController act as an endpoint thereby following the architectural style of REST.

While consuming an API an Http Request is sent and in return, a response is sent along with return data and an HTTP code. The HTTP Status Codes are important because they tell the consumer about what exactly happened to their request; a wrong HTTP code can confuse the consumer. A consumer should know (via a response) that its request has been taken care of or not, and if the response is not as expected, then the Status Code should tell the consumer where the problem is if it is a consumer level or at API level.

HTTP Status Codes

Level 200 (Success)	Level 400	Level 500
200 : OK	400 : Bad Request	500 : Internal Server Error
201 : Created	401 : Unauthorized	503 : Service Unavailable
203 : Non-Authoritative Information	403 : Forbidden	501 : Not Implemented
204 : No Content	404 : Not Found	504 : Gateway Timeout
	409 : Conflict	599 : Network timeout
		502 : Bad Gateway

GET

1. While the application is running that means our service is up. In the Postman, make a GET request for students by invoking the URL http://localhost:58278/api/students. When we click the Send button, we see that we get the data returned from the database for all the students added.

This URL will point to GetStudents() action of our controller and the URL is the outcome of the routing mechanism defined in Route.config file. In GetStudents() method the db.Students are returned that means all the students from the database returned as IQueryable.

```
private StudentManagementContext db = new StudentManagementContext();

// GET: api/Students
0 references
public IQueryable<Student> GetStudents()
{
    return db.Students;
}
```

```
1 reference
public class RouteConfig
{
    1 reference
    public static void RegisterRoutes(RouteCollection routes)
    {
        routes.IgnoreRoute("{resource}.axd/{*pathInfo}");

        routes.MapRoute(
            name: "Default",
            url: "{controller}/{action}/{id}",
            defaults: new { controller = "Home", action = "Index", id = UrlParameter.Optional }
        );
    }
}
```

2. One can invoke the endpoint to get the details of a single student from the database by passing his ID.

The GetStudent(int id) method takes student id as a parameter and returns the student from the database with status code 200 and student entity. If not found the method returns "Not Found" response i.e. 404.

```
// GET: api/Students/5
[ResponseType(typeof(Student))]
0 references
public IHttpActionResult GetStudent(int id)
{
    Student student = db.Students.Find(id);
    if (student == null)
    {
        return NotFound();
    }

    return Ok(student);
}
```

POST

 We can perform POST operation to add a new student to the database. To do that, in the Postman, select the HTTP verb as POST and URL as http://localhost:58278/api/students. During POST for creating the student, we need to provide student details which we want to add. So, provide the details in the JSON form, since we only have Id and Name of the student in Student entity, we'll provide that. Providing the Id is not mandatory here as the Id generated for the new student will be generated at the time of creation of student in the database and doesn't matter what Id you supply via request because Id is identity column in the database and would be incremented by 1 whenever a new entity is added. Provide the JSON for a new student under the Body section of the request.

Before sending the request, we also need to set the header information for the content type. So, add a new key in Headers section of the request with name "Content-Type" and value as "application/json". There are more keys that you can set in the headers section based on need. For e.g., if we would have been using a secure API, we would need to pass the Authorization header information like the type of authorization and token. We are not using secure API here, so providing content type information will suffice. Set the header information and click on Send to invoke the request.

Once the request is made, it is routed to PostStudent(Student student) method in the controller that is expecting Student entity as a parameter. It gets the entity that we passed in the Body section of the request. The property names for the JSON in the request should be the same as the property names in our entity. Once the Post method is executed, it creates the student in the database and sends back the id of the newly created student with the route information to access that student details.

```csharp
// POST: api/Students
[ResponseType(typeof(Student))]
0 references
public IHttpActionResult PostStudent(Student student)
{
    if (!ModelState.IsValid)
    {
        return BadRequest(ModelState);
    }

    db.Students.Add(student);
    db.SaveChanges();

    return CreatedAtRoute("DefaultApi", new { id = student.Id }, student);
}
```

After the POST method is executed, check the Students table in the database and we see a new Student with the name John got created.

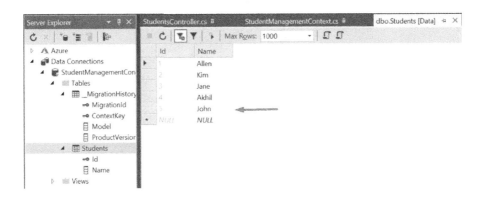

PUT

Put HTTP verb is basically used to update the existing record in the database or any update operation that you need to perform. For e.g. if we need to update a record I the database, say student name "Akhil" to "Akhil Mittal", we can perform PUT operation.

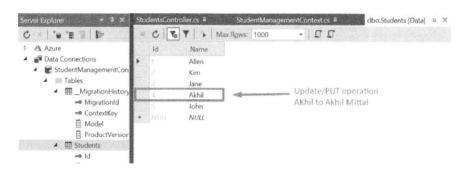

Select the HTTP verb as PUT in the request. In the URL, provide the Id of the student that you want to update and now in the body section, provide the details, such as the updated name of the student. In our case "Akhil Mittal".

Set the Content-type header and send the request.

| PUT ∨ | http://localhost:58278/api/students/4 | | Params | Send ∨ | Save ∨ |

Authorization   **Headers (1)**   Body ●   Pre-request Script   Tests   Code

Key	Value	Description	... Bulk Edit Presets ▾
☑ Content-Type	application/json		

Once the request is sent, it is routed to mapped **PutStudent()** action method of the API controller which takes id and student entity parameter. The method first checks that are the model passed is valid? if not it returns HTTP code 400 i.e. Bad request. If the model is valid, it matches the id passed in the model with the student id and if they do not match, it again sends the bad request. If model and id are fine, it changes the state of the model to be modified so that Entity Framework knows that this entity needs to be updated and then save changes to commit the changes to the database.

```
[ResponseType(typeof(void))]
0 references
public IHttpActionResult PutStudent(int id, Student student)
{
    if (!ModelState.IsValid)
    {
        return BadRequest(ModelState);
    }

    if (id != student.Id)
    {
        return BadRequest();
    }

    db.Entry(student).State = EntityState.Modified;

    try
    {
        db.SaveChanges();
    }
    catch (DbUpdateConcurrencyException)
    {
```

Check the database and the student name with id 4 is now updated to "Akhil Mittal". Earlier it was "Akhil".

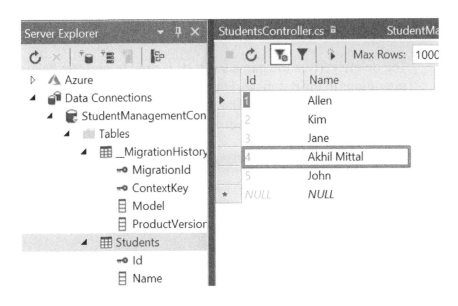

DELETE

The delete verb as the name suggests is used to perform delete operations in the database. For e.g., if we need to delete a record in the database, like deleting the student "John" from the database, we can make use of this HTTP verb.

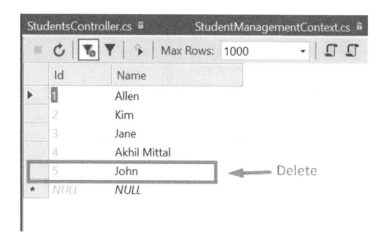

Set the HTTP verb as DELETE in the request and pass the student id that needs to be deleted in the URL for e.g. 5 to delete "John". Set the content type and send the request.

The request is automatically routed to the **DeleteStudent()** action method of the API controller due to the name of the action. The method takes an id parameter to delete the student. The method first performs the get operation for the student with the id passed. If a student is not found, it sends back the error NotFound() i.e. 404. If the student is found, it removes the found student from the list of all students and then saves changes to commit the changes to the database. It returns OK i.e. 200 status code in the response after a successful transaction.

```
// DELETE: api/Students/5
[ResponseType(typeof(Student))]
0 references
public IHttpActionResult DeleteStudent(int id)
{
    Student student = db.Students.Find(id);
    if (student == null)
    {
        return NotFound();
    }

    db.Students.Remove(student);
    db.SaveChanges();

    return Ok(student);
}
```

Check the database and we see the student with id 5 is deleted.

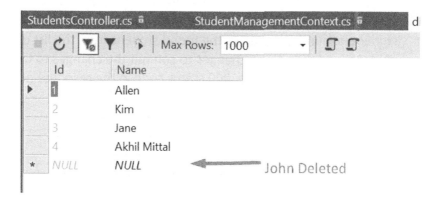

So, our delete operation also worked fine as expected.

In this section, we learned how to create a basic Web API project in visual studio and how to write basic CRUD operations with the help of Entity Framework. The concept could be utilized in big enterprise level applications where you can make use of other Web API features like content negotiation, filtering, attribute routing, exception handling, security, and logging. On the other hand, one can leverage the Entity Framework's features like various other approaches of data access, loadings, etc.

Entity Framework Core

EF Core is also an ORM, but it's not an upgrade to Entity Framework 6, and it shouldn't be regarded as such. Instead, Entity Framework Core is a lightweight, extensible, and cross-platform version of Entity Framework. Therefore, it comes with a bunch of new features and improvements over Entity Framework 6, and it's currently at version 2. For ASP.NET Core 1, version 1 should be used, and for ASP.NET Core 2, version 2 is advised. Entity Framework does not support all the features of Entity Framework 6. Entity Framework Core is recommended for new apps that don't require the heavy set of features Entity Framework 6 offers, or for apps that target .NET Core. It comes with a set of providers which could be used with a variety of databases. It could be used with Microsoft SQL Server, of course, but also with SQLite, Postgres, SQL Server Compact Edition, MySQL, and IBM DB2. And there's also an in-memory provider for testing purposes. EF Core can be used both for a code-first approach, which will create the database from the code, or a database-first approach, which is convenient if the database is already there. The following section will show the basic implementation of Entity Framework Core in a console application and of course, it could be used in any type of .Net application like MVC, Web API, Windows which needs to interact with the database. We'll start out by adding EF Core it to our project. We'll also investigate migrations, a way to migrate between different versions of our underlying datastore. We'll also check out how we can seed the database with data from code. Let's dive in by introducing Entity Framework Core.

Where can EF Core be Used

Entity Framework Core runs on .NET Core, and .NET Core runs in a lot of places. It runs inside of the full .NET Framework that is any version that is 4.5.1 or newer, and .NET Core itself can run on the CoreCLR, that's the runtime, and CoreCLR can run natively, not only in Windows but also on Mac and Linux. And the other place you can use EF Core on the Universal Windows Platform, or UWP for Windows 10, so that runs on any device or PC that can run Windows 10, but that doesn't necessarily mean you should use Entity Framework Core in all of these scenarios, and that's a really important point to keep in mind because Entity Framework Core is a brand new set of APIs, it doesn't have all of the features that you might be used to with Entity Framework 6, and while some of those features will be coming in future versions of EF Core, there are a few that will never be part of Entity Framework Core, so it's important to understand that, and that you may not want to start every single new project with the Entity Framework Core. Be sure that Entity Framework Core has the features that you need. If you want to target cross-platform or UWP, you have to use Entity Framework Core, but for .NET apps, you can still use Entity Framework 6, and in fact for ASP.NET Core apps that will definitely stay on Windows, in other words on a Windows Server, you can still build separate APIs using full .NET with the Entity Framework 6, and just have your ASP.NET Core app talk to that Entity Framework 6-based library.

Code First Approach using Entity Framework Core

Data access approaches are same in Entity Framework 6 and Entity Framework Core apart from some of the new features that EF Core provides. There are minor differences and implementation techniques that come along with the related packages. Let's see the EF Core in action step by step using code first approach. We'll cover more topics like data annotations and other migration techniques while walking through the practical implementation.

Adding Entities

1. Like explained, for code first approach, the application should have entities that would eventually result in the database tables. So, create a console application to start within .Net Framework 4.6.2. Name the application EmployeeManagement and solution name as EFCore.

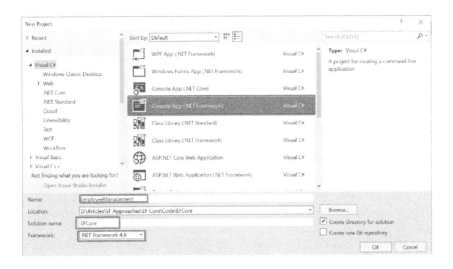

2. Add two entity classes one named Department and other as Employee. There would be one to many relationships between department and employee i.e. a department can have multiple employees and an employee would be associated with any one department.

Department:

```
Department.cs + X Program.cs
EmployeeManagement                            EmployeeManar       Departmentid
   3    using System.Linq;
   4    using System.Text;
   5    using System.Threading.Tasks;
   6
   7   namespace EmployeeManagement
   8   {
            0 references
   9        public class Department
  10        {
                0 references
  11            public int DepartmentId { get; set; }
                0 references
  12            public string DepartmentName { get; set; }
                0 references
  13            public string DepartmentDescription { get; set; }
  14        }
  15   }
  16
```

Solution Explorer
Search Solution Explorer (Ctrl+;)
- Solution 'EFCore' (1 project)
  - EmployeeManagement
    - Properties
    - References
    - App.config
    - Department.cs
    - Program.cs

Employee:

```
namespace EmployeeManagement
{
    0 references
    public class Employee
    {
        0 references
        public int EmployeeId { get; set; }
        0 references
        public string EmployeeName { get; set; }
        0 references
        public int DepartmentId { get; set; }

        0 references
        public virtual Department Departments { get; set; }
    }
}
```

3. The department entity has department name and description property and the entity employee has EmployeeId, Name and DepartmentId property that acts as a navigation property for departments. Add a property Employees denoting the collection of employees in Department entity as the department can have many employees. Similarly, a property of type Department is added in Employee class that returns a single department and not the list.

```csharp
namespace EmployeeManagement
{
    1 reference
    public class Department
    {
        0 references
        public int DepartmentId { get; set; }
        0 references
        public string DepartmentName { get; set; }
        0 references
        public string DepartmentDescription { get; set; }

        0 references
        public virtual ICollection<Employee> Employees { get; set; }
    }
}
```

Data Annotations

1. By giving the class an ID with name Id, this field is automatically regarded as the primary key. DepartmentId, i.e., the class name, followed by ID would be possible as well. If we would name this differently, the convention doesn't apply. But we can apply the key data annotation from System.ComponentModel.DataAnnotations. Personally, I like to apply the key annotation anyway, even if convention would ensure this property would be regarded as primary key, I feel it makes Entity classes so much more understandable at first glance. But, well, I've got the same gripe with a lot of convention-based approaches, so this is totally up to you. Following is the way in which you can add a [Key] for the property you want to make a primary key.

```csharp
using System;
using System.Collections.Generic;
using System.ComponentModel.DataAnnotations;
using System.Linq;
using System.Text;
using System.Threading.Tasks;

namespace EmployeeManagement
{
    1 reference
    public class Department
    {
        [Key]
        public int DepartmentId { get; set; }
        0 references
        public string DepartmentName { get; set; }
        0 references
        public string DepartmentDescription { get; set; }

        0 references
        public virtual ICollection<Employee> Employees { get; set; }

    }
}
```

2. Similarly, add the key for EmployeeId i.e. a primary key for Employee entity.

```csharp
using System;
using System.Collections.Generic;
using System.ComponentModel.DataAnnotations;
using System.Linq;
using System.Text;
using System.Threading.Tasks;

namespace EmployeeManagement
{
    1 reference
    public class Employee
    {
        [Key]
        0 references
        public int EmployeeId { get; set; }
        0 references
        public string EmployeeName { get; set; }
        0 references
        public int DepartmentId { get; set; }

        0 references
        public virtual Department Departments { get; set; }
    }
}
```

3. Another thing of importance is a generation of ID primary keys. By convention, primary keys that are of integer or GUID data type will be set up to have their values generated on add. In other words, our ID will be an identity column. To explicitly state this, we can use another annotation, the database-generated annotation from the **System.ComponentModel.DataAnnotations.SchemaNamespace**. It has three possible values,

- null for no generation,
- identity for generation on add, and
- computed for generation on add or update.

We need the identity option. A new key will be generated when an Employee is added. How this value is generated depends on the database provider being used. Database providers may automatically set up value generation for some property types, while others will require you to manually set up how the value is generated. In our case, we'll be using SQL Server. So, we're good to go. A new integer primary key will be automatically generated without further setup

```
using System;
using System.Collections.Generic;
using System.ComponentModel.DataAnnotations;
using System.ComponentModel.DataAnnotations.Schema;
using System.Linq;
using System.Text;
using System.Threading.Tasks;

namespace EmployeeManagement
{
    1 reference
    public class Employee
    {
        [Key]
        [DatabaseGenerated(DatabaseGeneratedOption.Identity)]
        0 references
        public int EmployeeId { get; set; }
```

4. We want to signify the relationship between Department and Employee. If we look back at the Department entity, we already defined a collection of Employee, but we want to navigate through our object graph from a point of interest to the parent department. So, we need a property to refer to that parent department. And we need to state what the foreign key property will be. Again, there's a convention-based and an explicit approach possible. By convention, a relationship will be created when there is a navigation property discovered on a type. And a property is considered a navigation property if the type it points to cannot be mapped as a scalar type by the current database provider. So, if we add a property Department of type Department, this is considered the navigation property, and a relationship will be created. Relationships that are discovered by convention will always target the primary key of the principal entity. And in this case, that's the ID of the Department. That will be our foreign key. It's not required to explicitly define this foreign key property on the dependent class. And the dependent class, well, that's our Employee class. But it is recommended, so we'll add one. So that's the convention-based approach. If we do not want the convention-based approach to be followed, which states that a foreign key will be named according to the navigation property's class name followed by id, so DepartmentId in our case, we can again use an annotation for that. The foreign key annotation from the **System.ComponentModel.DataAnnotations.Schema** namespace.

```csharp
using System;
using System.Collections.Generic;
using System.ComponentModel.DataAnnotations;
using System.ComponentModel.DataAnnotations.Schema;
using System.Linq;
using System.Text;
using System.Threading.Tasks;

namespace EmployeeManagement
{
    1 reference
    public class Employee
    {
        [Key]
        [DatabaseGenerated(DatabaseGeneratedOption.Identity)]
        0 references
        public int EmployeeId { get; set; }
        0 references
        public string EmployeeName { get; set; }
        0 references
        public int DepartmentId { get; set; }

        [ForeignKey("DepartmentId")]
        0 references
        public virtual Department Department { get; set; }
    }
}
```

5. The entity classes properties do not have any data annotation w.r.t mandatories or max lengths. If we leave our entity classes like this, our database columns will allow null for fields that should not be null. And we'll be off max and varchar length instead of a specific maximum size. It's best practice to ensure these field restrictions are applied at the lowest possible level. So, in our case, that's the database itself. This ensures the best possible integrity. So, let's apply these attributes. For Employee, the EmployeeName was required with a maxLength of 50. And for the Department entity, we want these as well. Let's make Name required with a maximum length of 50.

```csharp
using System;
using System.Collections.Generic;
using System.ComponentModel.DataAnnotations;
using System.ComponentModel.DataAnnotations.Schema;
using System.Linq;
using System.Text;
using System.Threading.Tasks;

namespace EmployeeManagement
{
    1 reference
    public class Employee
    {
        [Key]
        [DatabaseGenerated(DatabaseGeneratedOption.Identity)]
        0 references
        public int EmployeeId { get; set; }

        [Required]
        [MaxLength(50)]
        0 references
        public string EmployeeName { get; set; }
        0 references
        public int DepartmentId { get; set; }

        [ForeignKey("DepartmentId")]
        0 references
        public virtual Department Department { get; set; }
    }
}
```

Adding DB Context

In this section, we'll create a context to interact with our database and that context represents a session with the database, and it can be used to query and save instances of our entities. Our entity classes are just classes. We didn't need any extra dependencies to create those but the DBContext, that's part of Entity Framework Core. And we'll also need a provider. In our case, we'll use the SQL Server provider, so we can connect to a LocalDB instance.

1. Let's open the NuGet dialog. Right click on the project and select "Manage NuGet Packages…" option.

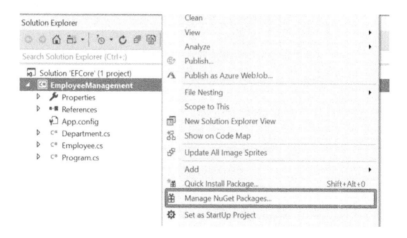

2. We want to look for the Microsoft.EntityFrameworkCore.SqlServer package. If we install that, the Entity Framework core dependencies will be added as well, so we'll have all we need for now.

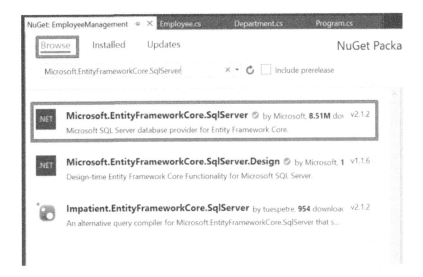

3. Select the latest stable version and click install.

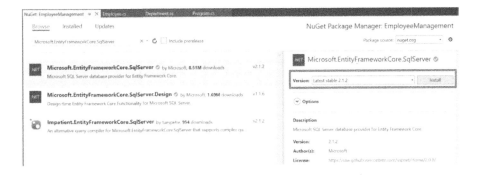

4.   Accept the license agreement.

As you can guess by now, no need to do this when you're on ASP.NET Core 2 and you've referenced the Microsoft.AspNetCore.All package. That includes the necessary references for Entity Framework Core.

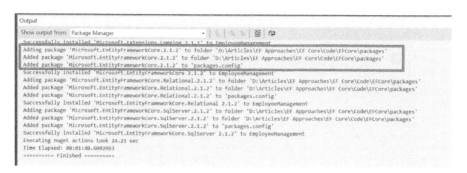

5. Now let's add a new class, EmployeeManagementContext.

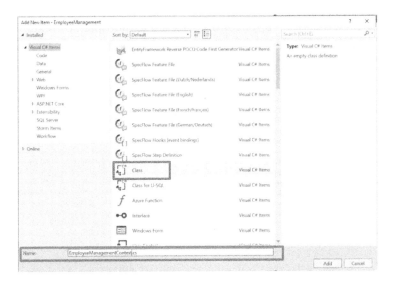

6. Have the class inherit DBContext. DBContext can be found in the **Microsoft.EntityFrameworkCore** namespace. Bigger applications often use multiple contexts. For example, were we to add some sort of reporting module to our application, that would fit in a separate context. There's no need for all the entities that map to tables in a database to be in the same context. Multiple contexts can work on the same database. In our case, well, we only have two entities, so one context is sufficient.

```csharp
using System;
using System.Collections.Generic;
using System.Linq;
using System.Text;
using System.Threading.Tasks;

namespace EmployeeManagement
{
    0 references
    public class EmployeeManagementContext : DbContext
    {

    }
}
```

DbContext (in Microsoft.EntityFrameworkCore)
DbContextErrorEventData (in Microsoft.EntityFrameworkCore.Diagnostics)
DbContextEventData (in Microsoft.EntityFrameworkCore.Diagnostics)
DbContextFactoryOptions (in Microsoft.EntityFrameworkCore.Infrastructure)
DbContextOptions (in Microsoft.EntityFrameworkCore)

7. In this context, we now want to define DbSets for our entities. Such a DbSet can be used to query and save instances of its entity type. LINQ queries against a DbSet will be translated into queries against the database. Add two properties each for entity classes that we have returning DbSet of the entity.

```csharp
0 references
public class EmployeeManagementContext : DbContext
{
    0 references
    public DbSet<Employee> Employees { get; set; }
    0 references
    public DbSet<Department> Departments { get; set; }
}
```

8. How do we tell the context that which database it has to associate to? Well, that's through a connection string. We need to provide this connection string to our DBContext. In other words, we need to configure this DBContext. And there are essentially two ways of doing this. Let's open our EmployeeManagementContext again. The first way of doing this is through overriding the OnConfigure method on the DBContext. This has an optionsBuilder as a parameter. And that optionsBuilder provides us with a method-- UseSqlServer. This tells the DBContext it's being used to connect to a SQL server database, and it's here that we can provide a connection string. So that's one way.

```
0 references
protected override void OnConfiguring(DbContextOptionsBuilder optionsBuilder)
{
    optionsBuilder.UseSqlServer("connectionstring");
    base.OnConfiguring(optionsBuilder);
}
```

9. But let's look at the other way--via the constructor. So, let's comment OnConfiguring out, and have a look at the DBContext definition. The DBContext exposes a constructor that accepts DBContext options.

```
public class DbContext : IDisposable, IInfrastructure<IServiceProvider>, IDbContextDepend
{
    //
    // Summary:
    //     Initializes a new instance of the Microsoft.EntityFrameworkCore.DbContext class
    //     using the specified options. The Microsoft.EntityFrameworkCore.DbContext.OnConfig
    //     method will still be called to allow further configuration of the options.
    //
    // Parameters:
    //   options:
    //     The options for this context.
    public DbContext([NotNullAttribute] DbContextOptions options);
    protected DbContext();

    public virtual DatabaseFacade Database { get; }
    public virtual ChangeTracker ChangeTracker { get; }
    public virtual IModel Model { get; }

    public virtual EntityEntry Add([NotNullAttribute] object entity);
```

10. So, let's add a constructor that calls this constructor overload. What this allows us to do, and what isn't possible when overriding the OnConfigure method, is that we can provide options at the moment we register our DBContext. And that's a more logical approach.

```
public EmployeeManagementContext(DbContextOptions<EmployeeManagementContext> options) : base (options)
{

}
```

11. To get the instance of this context class now, let's add a new class named Initialize and add a static method responsible for returning context instance. The GetContext() method overload on these options, so we can use now-- **UseSqlServer**. It's from the **Microsoft.EntityFrameworkCore** namespace, so let's add that using statement. And in this method, we can pass in the connection string. So, let's add a variable to hold this connection string for now. The next logical question is, What would that connection string look like? Well, we're going to be using local DB, as this is installed automatically together with Visual Studio. But if you have a full SQL Server installation in your network, it'll work as well. Just make sure you change the connection string accordingly. The name (localdb)\MSSQLLocalDB is the default instance name, but it can be different on your machine depending on whatever you inputted on install. So, if you're not sure, have a look at the SQL Server Object Explorer window. If you don't see that on your machine, you can find it underneath the View menu item.

```
1 reference
public class Initialize
{
    1 reference
    public static EmployeeManagementContext GetContext()
    {
        var connectionString = @"Server=(localdb)\mssqllocaldb;Database=EmployeeManagementDB;Trusted_Connection=True;";
        DbContextOptionsBuilder<EmployeeManagementContext> options = new DbContextOptionsBuilder<EmployeeManagementContext>();
        options.UseSqlServer(connectionString);
        return new EmployeeManagementContext(options.Options);
    }
}
```

```
public class Initialize
    {
        public static EmployeeManagementContext
GetContext()
        {
            var connectionString =
@"Server=(localdb)\mssqllocaldb;Database=EmployeeMan
agementDB;Trusted_Connection=True;";

DbContextOptionsBuilder<EmployeeManagementContext>
options = new
DbContextOptionsBuilder<EmployeeManagementContext>()
;
            options.UseSqlServer(connectionString);
            return new
EmployeeManagementContext(options.Options);
        }
    }
```

12. Call the GetContext() method to create the instance of context class in Program.cs. Ideally, when we run the application and instance of context class get created, the database should be ready at local db.

```
using System;
using System.Collections.Generic;
using System.Linq;
using System.Text;
using System.Threading.Tasks;

namespace EmployeeManagement
{
    0 references
    class Program
    {
        0 references
        static void Main(string[] args)
        {
            var context = Initialize.GetContext();
        }
    }
}
```

13. This is a code-first approach for a new database, so the database should be generated if it doesn't exist yet. Let's open our EmployeeManagementContext again to make sure that happens. To the constructor that will be used when requesting an instance from the container through dependency injection, we call EnsureCreated() on the database object. This database is an object is defined on DBContext. If the database already exists, nothing will happen, but if it doesn't, this call ensures it is effectively created.

Context constructor:

```
public
EmployeeManagementContext(DbContextOptions<EmployeeM
anagementContext> options) : base (options){
                Database.Migrate();
        }
```

14. Run the application. Once the application is run and Program.cs's main method executes the GetContext() method, let's open that SQL Object Explorer window again. Let's refresh the database list from our MSSQLLocalDB instance. And it looks like our EmployeeManagementDB data is there. Let's have a look at the tables. Apparently, two tables have been created, a Departments and an Employee table, the pluralized names of our entities.

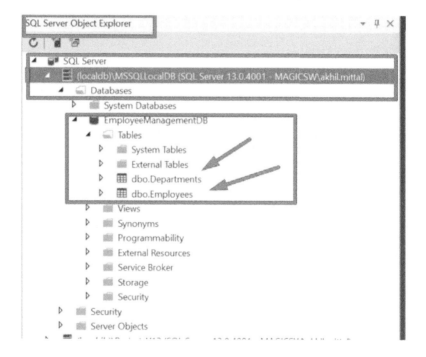

15. The Departments table has a primary key, DepartmentId, a DepartmentName with a maximum length of 50, which cannot be null. If you look at the Department entity, we see that the column definition matches the definition of the fields on our Department entity. Let's have a look at the Employees table. It has a DepartmentId, which is a foreign key, and it has an EmployeeName field, which is required, thus cannot be null, and a maximum length of 50. So that matches our Employee entity. The attributes we applied to the properties on our entity classes were, thus, taken into account. So far, so good. But this is only one way of doing this.

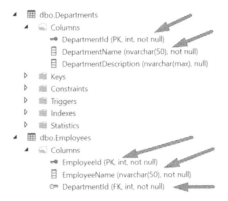

If we work like this, we work by ensuring the database is created by calling Database.EnsureCreated(). But if we do that, well, we're forgetting something. Just as code evolves, a database evolves as well. Let's look into migrations to see how we can improve on what we've done up until now and how we can handle an evolving database.

Code First Migrations in EF Core

Just as our code evolves, so does the database. New tables might be added after a while, existing tables might be dropped or altered. Migrations allow us to provide code to change the database from one version to another. They're an important part of almost all applications, so let's look into it. What we are going to do, we are going to use migrations to create the initial database version, version 1. So, we'll replace what we did in the previous demo by this new and better approach. The reason is that by doing that, we'll have code in place to start from no database at all, rather than having to provide an already existing one. Then, we'll add another migration to migrate to a new version, version 2. To allow for something like this, we'll first need to create an initial snapshot of our database. In the Entity Framework core world, this is achieved with tooling, so we'll have to add these tools first. And these tools are essentially just another set of dependencies that add commands we can execute.

1.   Let's add the package Microsoft.EntityFrameworkCore.Tools.

2. So, then we'll have to create that initial snapshot or migration of our database and schema. For that, we have to be able to execute one of the commands we just enabled. And executing those commands, well, you can do that in the package manager console. If you don't currently see that, you can get it via Tools, NuGet Package Manager, Package Manager Console.

3. The command we're looking for is the Add-Migration command. It expects a name for the migration we're going to add. So, let's say we want to name it EmployeeManagementInitialMigration.

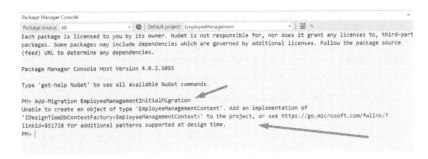

4. It gives us the error that it cannot create the object of type EmployeeManagementContext and asks us to add an implementation of IDesignTimeContextFactory. So, let's create a new class named DesignTimeContextFactory inheriting from IDesignTimeDbContextFactory of our context class and add te CreateDbContext method which creates optionsBuilder and returns the context class instance with these options as a parameter.

```
 7   using Microsoft.EntityFrameworkCore;
 8   using Microsoft.EntityFrameworkCore.Design;
 9   using Microsoft.Extensions.Configuration;
10
11 □namespace EmployeeManagement
12   {
           0 references
13       public class DesignTimeDbContextFactory : IDesignTimeDbContextFactory<EmployeeManagementContext>
14       {
               0 references
15           public EmployeeManagementContext CreateDbContext(string[] args)
16           {
17               var optionsBuilder = new DbContextOptionsBuilder<EmployeeManagementContext>();
18               optionsBuilder.UseSqlServer(@"Server=(localdb)\mssqllocaldb;Database=EmployeeManagementDB;Trusted_Connection=True;");
19
20               return new EmployeeManagementContext(optionsBuilder.Options);
21           }
22       }
23   }
```

Code:

```
using System;
using System.Collections.Generic;
using System.IO;
using System.Linq;
using System.Text;
using System.Threading.Tasks;
using Microsoft.EntityFrameworkCore;
using Microsoft.EntityFrameworkCore.Design;
using Microsoft.Extensions.Configuration;

namespace EmployeeManagement
{
```

```csharp
    public class DesignTimeDbContextFactory :
IDesignTimeDbContextFactory<EmployeeManagementContext>
    {
        public EmployeeManagementContext
CreateDbContext(string[] args)
        {
            var optionsBuilder = new
DbContextOptionsBuilder<EmployeeManagementContext>();

optionsBuilder.UseSqlServer(@"Server=(localdb)\mssql
localdb;Database=EmployeeManagementDB;Trusted_Connec
tion=True;");

            return new
EmployeeManagementContext(optionsBuilder.Options);
        }
    }
}
```

5. Now run the Add-Migration command i.e.
    Add-Migration EmployeeManagementInitialMigration

```
PM> Add-Migration EmployeeManagementInitialMigration
Unable to create an object of type 'EmployeeManagementContext'. Add an implementation of 'IDesignTimeDbContextFactory<EmployeeManagementContext>' to the
project, or see https://go.microsoft.com/fwlink/?linkid=851728 for additional patterns supported at design time.
PM> Add-Migration EmployeeManagementInitialMigration
To undo this action, use Remove-Migration.
PM>
```

If we look at our solution now, we see there's a new Migrations folder. And it contains two files. One, a snapshot of our current context model.

Let's have a look at that.

6. This contains the current model as we defined through our entities, including the annotations we provided. We can find our Department entity and our Employee entity. And at the end of the file, the relation between Department and Employee.

```
[DbContext(typeof(EmployeeManagementContext))]
0 references
partial class EmployeeManagementContextModelSnapshot : ModelSnapshot
{
    0 references
    protected override void BuildModel(ModelBuilder modelBuilder)
    {
#pragma warning disable 612, 618
        modelBuilder
            .HasAnnotation("ProductVersion", "2.1.2-rtm-30932")
            .HasAnnotation("Relational:MaxIdentifierLength", 128)
            .HasAnnotation("SqlServer:ValueGenerationStrategy", SqlServerValueGenerationStrategy.IdentityColumn);

        modelBuilder.Entity("EmployeeManagement.Department", b =>
            {
                b.Property<int>("DepartmentId")
                    .ValueGeneratedOnAdd()
                    .HasAnnotation("SqlServer:ValueGenerationStrategy", SqlServerValueGenerationStrategy.IdentityColumn);

                b.Property<string>("DepartmentDescription");

                b.Property<string>("DepartmentName")
                    .IsRequired()
                    .HasMaxLength(50);

                b.HasKey("DepartmentId");

                b.ToTable("Departments");
            });

        modelBuilder.Entity("EmployeeManagement.Employee", b =>
            {
                b.Property<int>("EmployeeId")
                    .ValueGeneratedOnAdd()
                    .HasAnnotation("SqlServer:ValueGenerationStrategy", SqlServerValueGenerationStrategy.IdentityColumn);
```

7.   The second file we see is the EmployeeManagement
     InitialMigration. That's the name we just gave to our migration.
     This contains the code needed by the migration builder to build
     this version of the database, both Up (from current to the new
     version) and Down (from this version to the previous version). If
     we look at Up, we see two CreateTable statements and a
     CreateIndex statement. That means it's starting from no
     database at all, and this migration contains the code to build
     the initial database. And if we look at Down, we see what
     should happen to end up with an empty database--two
     DropTable statements.

```
namespace EmployeeManagement.Migrations
{
    1 reference
    public partial class EmployeeManagementInitialMigration : Migration
    {
        0 references
        protected override void Up(MigrationBuilder migrationBuilder)
        {
            migrationBuilder.CreateTable(
                name: "Departments",
                columns: table => new
                {
                    DepartmentId = table.Column<int>(nullable: false)
                        .Annotation("SqlServer:ValueGenerationStrategy", SqlServerValueGenerationStrategy.IdentityColumn),
                    DepartmentName = table.Column<string>(maxLength: 50, nullable: false),
                    DepartmentDescription = table.Column<string>(nullable: true)
                },
                constraints: table =>
                {
                    table.PrimaryKey("PK_Departments", x => x.DepartmentId);
                });

            migrationBuilder.CreateTable(
                name: "Employees",
                columns: table => new
                {
                    EmployeeId = table.Column<int>(nullable: false)
                        .Annotation("SqlServer:ValueGenerationStrategy", SqlServerValueGenerationStrategy.IdentityColumn),
                    EmployeeName = table.Column<string>(maxLength: 50, nullable: false),
                    DepartmentId = table.Column<int>(nullable: false)
                },
                constraints: table =>
                {
                    table.PrimaryKey("PK_Employees", x => x.EmployeeId);
                    table.ForeignKey(
```

If new migrations are added, new files like this will be created,
and by executing them in order our database can evolve
together with our code. By the way, you don't need to run the
Add-Migration command to generate these files. We could've

written them by hand. And that might still be feasible for one or two or three tables maybe. But it's definitely not something you want to do for a larger database. So, these tools are quite helpful. So far, so good.

8. There's one more thing we have to do. We have to ensure that the migration is effectively applied to our database. And there's another command for that. It's called the update-database command. If we execute this, the migrations will be applied to our current database. Rather than doing it from command, I'll show you how we can do this from code.

```
Package Manager Console
Package source: All          ▼  ⚙  Default project  EmployeeManagement        ▼  ≡
Package Manager Console Host Version 4.6.2.5055

Type 'get-help NuGet' to see all available NuGet commands.

PM> Add-Migration EmployeeManagementInitialMigration
Unable to create an object of type 'EmployeeManagementContext'. Add an implementation of
'IDesignTimeDbContextFactory<EmployeeManagementContext>' to the project, or see https://go.microsoft.com/fwlink/?linkid=851728 for
additional patterns supported at design time.
PM> Add-Migration EmployeeManagementInitialMigration
To undo this action, use Remove-Migration.
PM> Update-Migrations  ◄───────────────     X
```

9. Let's open the context again. What we can do is replace Database.EnsureCreated() by Database.Migrate(). This will execute migrations, which, if there's no database yet, will create it. And that's really all we have to do. But as said, we're replacing what we did in the previous clip because, well, most applications do require migrations. And for those, it's a good idea to start from no database at all if you have the chance.

```
namespace EmployeeManagement
{
    12 references
    public class EmployeeManagementContext : DbContext
    {
        2 references
        public EmployeeManagementContext(DbContextOptions<EmployeeManagementContext> options) : base (option
        {
            Database.Migrate();
        }
        0 references
        public DbSet<Employee> Employees { get; set; }
        0 references
```

10. So, what we want to do is remove the current database first. If we don't do that, this call will try and apply the migrations, i.e., create the Departments and Employees tables, and that will fail because they already exist. In the SQL Server Object Explorer, right-click the existing database and delete it.

If you do want to provide an existing database, you can follow the same flow we just did, but delete the first migration file. Generally speaking, though, that's not a good place to be unless your application must start from an existing database. Let's give this a try.

11. Run the application.

```
 9      class Program
10      {
            0 references
11          static void Main(string[] args)        Run the application
12
13              var context = Initialize.GetContext();
14          }
15      }
16  }
17
```

12. Let's have a look at our localDB server. Let's refresh the databases list. Our database was created again, but by working like this instead of how we did it previously, we've ensured our database can migrate from not existing at all to its initial version and upcoming versions after that. A better approach than what we did in the previous sections. Let's have a look at the database itself.

It now contains an additional table--_EFMigrationsHistory. Let's have a look at what's in there. Entity Framework Core uses this table in the database to keep track of which migrations have already been applied to the database.

This ensures that that Database.Migrate() call, or alternatively, the Update-Database call from the command line doesn't try to execute the same migrations over and over again.

13. Let's continue with adding a new migration. An Employee doesn't seem to have a salary. We may have missed that on purpose because this allows us to look into an additional migration. So, let's add that Salary property.

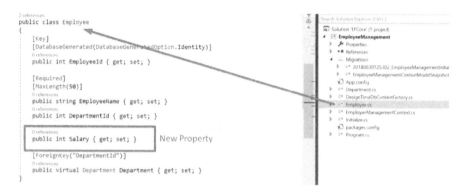

14. Then, let's execute the Add-Migration command again so the file gets generated for us. Let's name this migration EmployeeManagementAddSalaryToEmployee.

Our Migrations folder now includes a new file.

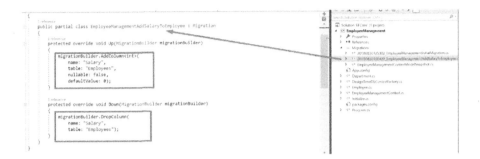

And if looking at this file, we see that the Up method contains the code to add the Salary column, and the Down method contains the code to drop the column again.

15. Let's run the application again.

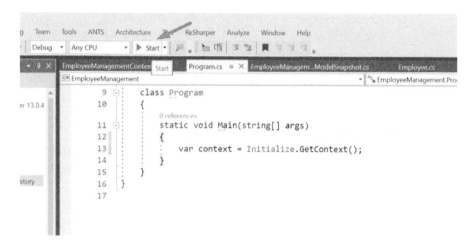

16. Let's have a quick look at the database. Employees now indeed contain a Salary column.

17. Let's have a look at that EFMigrationHistory table. And, indeed, it also contains the new migration. And that's how we can work with migrations to migrate our database from one version to another. But if we look at the data that's in these tables, we see there's nothing there yet. No Employees, Department. To add data to start with, we should seed the database. Let's see in the next section how we can do that.

Seeding the Database

We still haven't got data in our database. It would be nice to have some to test with. That principle, providing your database with data to start with, is called seeding the database. It's often used to provide master data. We saw how we do that in EF 6 versions. Here we'll discuss another approach to seed the database.

1. We'll write an extension method on our context. So, let's start with that extension method. Let's add a new class, EmployeeManagementContextExtensions. Let's make it static.

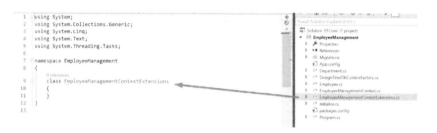

2. Let's add one static method to it, EnsureSeedDataForContext. The method has one parameter of type EmployeeManagementContext named context, and it's decorated with this, which tells the compiler it extends EmployeeManagementContext. The first thing we want to do is check if the database already contains our sample data. We want to insert departments and their employees. So, let's check if the Departments table is empty. An employee can't exist without a department, so that's sufficient. If it's not empty, we already have data in there, and we don't want to insert additional data. And, otherwise, we can start adding data. We first create a Department with the name "Technology" and provide three employees (Jack, Kim, Shen) to that department.

We do not provide IDs as these are now auto-generated by the database. Then we'll want to add these to the context. For that, we can use Add method or AddRange method if there are multiple departments on the Departments DBSet on our context. And from this moment on, the entities are tracked by the context. But they aren't inserted yet. For that, we must call SaveChanges on the context. Calling SaveChanges on the context will effectively execute the statements on our database.

```csharp
0 references
public static void EnsureSeedDataForContext(this EmployeeManagementContext context)
{
    if (context.Departments.Any())
    {
        return;
    }

    Department department = new Department
    {
        DepartmentName = "Technology",
        Employees = new List<Employee>
        {
            new Employee() {EmployeeName = "Jack"},
            new Employee() {EmployeeName = "Kim"},
            new Employee() {EmployeeName = "Shen"}
        }
    };

    context.Departments.Add(department);

    Employee employee = new Employee
    {
        EmployeeName = "Akhil Mittal",
        DepartmentId = 1
    };

    context.Employees.Add(employee);
    context.SaveChanges();
}
```

Code:

```csharp
using System;
using System.Collections.Generic;
```

```csharp
using System.Linq;
using System.Text;
using System.Threading.Tasks;

namespace EmployeeManagement
{
    public static class
EmployeeManagementContextExtensions
    {
        public static void
EnsureSeedDataForContext(this
EmployeeManagementContext context)
        {
            if (context.Departments.Any())
            {
                return;
            }

            Department department = new Department
            {
                DepartmentName = "Technology",
                Employees = new List<Employee>
                {
                    new Employee() {EmployeeName =
"Jack"},

                    new Employee() {EmployeeName =
"Kim"},

                    new Employee() {EmployeeName =
"Shen"}
                }
            };

            context.Departments.Add(department);
```

```
Employee employee = new Employee
{
    EmployeeName = "Akhil Mittal",
    DepartmentId = 1
};

context.Employees.Add(employee);
context.SaveChanges();
        }
    }
}
```

And that's already it for the extension method. Then we need to execute this extension method.

3. Call the extension method EnsureSeedDataForContext() after you create the instance of the context in Program.cs class. Then run the application.

```
namespace EmployeeManagement
{
    0 references
    class Program
    {
        0 references
        static void Main(string[] args)
        {
            var context = Initialize.GetContext();
            context.EnsureSeedDataForContext();
        }
    }
}
```

4. Let's have a look at our database. And the Departments table contains sample data, and so does the Employees table. And with that, we now know what Entity Framework Core is, its most important concepts, and how to use those.

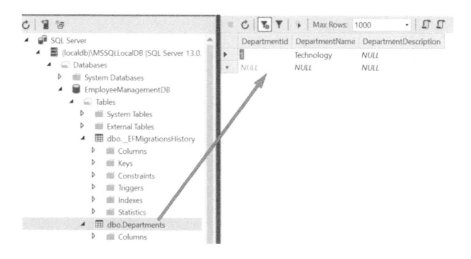

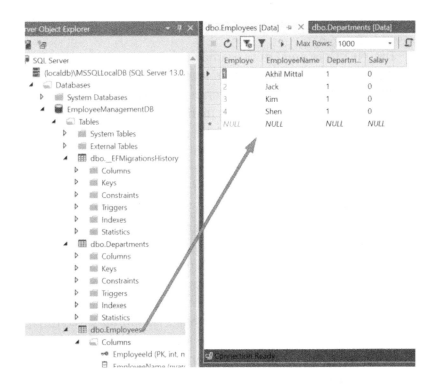

EF Core Summary

The .NET Core and Entity Framework Core are truly cross-platform, but they're cross-platform on two levels. You can run .NET Core apps using EF Core on any of these platforms, but you can also create, debug, and build them on any one of the platforms as well, and with this cross-platform tool, Visual Studio Code and all of its rich features, plus the fact that it is open source, I've got the ability to do that coding and debugging on any one of the platforms. Visual Studio Code only enhances the flexibility we have for working with .NET Core and Entity Framework Core, but EF Core itself is also flexible. You can also deploy these apps to Docker and run them anywhere that Docker runs. Entity Framework Core is a lightweight, extensible, and cross-platform version of Entity Framework. It's recommended for new applications that don't need the full Entity Framework 6 feature set and for .NET Core applications. We created entity classes first. We can use annotations on those to define things like primary and foreign keys, required fields, and so on. Those are then registered as DBSets on the DBContext. That context represents a session with the database. And it can be used to query and save instances of our entities. From that moment on, we could access our entities through LINQ. There was another important concept we looked into--migrations. Just as our code evolves, so does the database. New tables might be added. After a while, existing tables might be dropped or altered. Migrations allow us to provide code to change the database from one version to another. And, lastly, we investigated an option to seed the database providing it with data to start with.

Conclusion

This book on Entity Framework covered the most possible details of Entity Framework and Entity Framework Core, Since the intent was very much to explain the practical concepts and their implementations, few topics were beyond the scope of this book. The book started with the introduction of Entity Framework followed by why and where Entity Framework could be used. We discussed the EF architecture in detail and how it got built over legacy ADO.NET technology. We covered the three approaches of Entity Framework for data access in detail, looking closely into each detail with some practical examples which internally explained the concept of DbSets and DbContexts. Code first approach being so interesting and famous and most recommended for fresh applications was covered in detail with all the code first options and migrations as well. The book also covered topics like several ways of querying the database using Entity Framework and several types of loadings supported in EF. To understand the practical implementation of EF in a working application, the WebAPI section covered the detailed explanation and tutorial of using Entity Framework in Web API's that could similarly be used in MVC applications. We covered the endpoints of WebAPI and the HTTP operations associated with those in detail with practical examples. Last but not the least is the topic of Entity Framework Core, a light weighted version of Entity Framework. The book covered EF Core in detail with practical examples covering the topics like introduction to EF Core, its use in real time scenario, code first approach explaining the role of data annotations, migrations, and contexts. EF Core section covered another way to seed the database to provide master data to the generated tables and concluded with the summary of EF Core.

References

1. Entity Framework: Wikipedia
2. Getting Started with EF 6
3. Entity Framework Overview
4. Entity Framework Architecture
5. Building Your First API with ASP.NET Core

Index

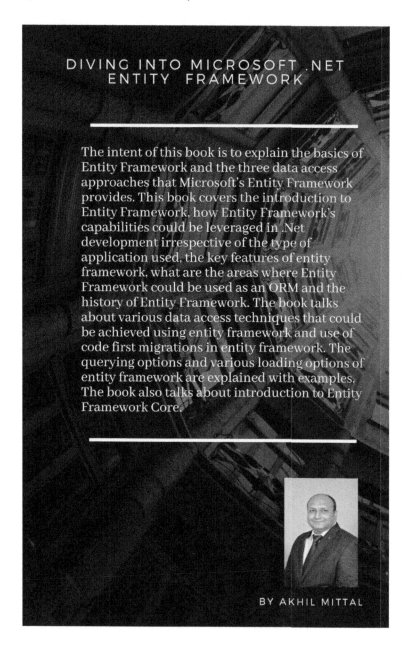

DIVING INTO MICROSOFT .NET
ENTITY FRAMEWORK

The intent of this book is to explain the basics of Entity Framework and the three data access approaches that Microsoft's Entity Framework provides. This book covers the introduction to Entity Framework, how Entity Framework's capabilities could be leveraged in .Net development irrespective of the type of application used, the key features of entity framework, what are the areas where Entity Framework could be used as an ORM and the history of Entity Framework. The book talks about various data access techniques that could be achieved using entity framework and use of code first migrations in entity framework. The querying options and various loading options of entity framework are explained with examples. The book also talks about introduction to Entity Framework Core.

BY AKHIL MITTAL

Printed in Great Britain
by Amazon

21789705R00128